Developing Vocabulary

ANNOTATED INSTRUCTOR'S EDITION

D. J. Henry
Daytona Beach Community College

Susan Pongratz
Thomas Nelson Community College

PEARSON
Longman

New York   Boston San Francisco
London Toronto Sydney Tokyo Singapore Madrid
Mexico City Munich Paris Cape Town Hong Kong Montreal

Acquisitions Editor: Melanie Craig
Development Editor: Susan Gouijnstook
Marketing Manager: Thomas DeMarco
Senior Supplements Editor: Donna Campion
Media Supplements Editor: Jenna Egan
Production Manager: Ellen MacElree
Project Coordination, Text Design, and Electronic Page Makeup: Nesbitt Graphics, Inc.
Cover Design Manager: Wendy Ann Fredericks
Cover Designer: Joe DePinho
Photo Researcher: Rona Tuccillo
Senior Manufacturing Buyer: Dennis J. Para
Printer and Binder: QuebecorWorld–Taunton
Cover Printer: Phoenix Color Corps

Library of Congress Cataloging-in-Publication Data on file with the Library of Congress

Please visit us at http://www.ablongman.com/vocabulary

ISBN 0-321-41070-X (Student Edition)

ISBN 0-321-43447-1 (Instructor's Edition)

1 2 3 4 5 6 7 8 9 10—WCT—09 08 07 06

Contents

UNIT 3
Vocabulary in Social Sciences

UNIT 4
Vocabulary in Math, Science, and Technology

Preface

Learning new vocabulary requires preparation and practice. Most students add 2,000 to 3,000 words each year to their reading vocabularies. A knowledge of vocabulary is closely tied to a student's reading comprehension, and college textbooks contain a great deal of specialized vocabulary; therefore, increasing your vocabulary through the study of context clues, word analysis, and dictionary practice will improve your ability to comprehend and communicate.

The chapters in this textbook contain features to provide several encounters with each new word to promote in-depth learning.

Getting Ready to Read About

Each chapter begins with an introduction that includes information about a college course and the word parts to help you understand the vocabulary of that subject area.

Vocabulary in Context

We learn most of our vocabulary by watching, listening, and reading, and you will discover in Chapter 1 that recognizing context clues will facilitate your learning. Therefore, unless you are directed to do so, please avoid using a dictionary. However, after you have completed the first exercise, turn to the partial answer key to check your answers.

Synonyms and Antonyms

Each chapter includes an exercise on synonyms and antonyms. Learning a one-word definition (synonym) and learning the opposite meaning (antonym) will provide practice with what the word is and what it is not.

Stop and Think

At the end of each chapter, you will find two exercises to help you learn the new words. Whether you are asked to use the words to write a summary or search online for additional information about the word, each activity is designed so that you can work alone or in a study group. Remember, if you encounter the word seven or eight times, you are more likely to remember its definition and the correct way to use it.

The Teaching and Learning Package

Longman is pleased to offer a variety of support materials to help make teaching vocabulary easier on teachers and to help students excel in their coursework. Contact your local Longman sales representative for more information on pricing and how to create a package.

An **Annotated Instructor's Edition (0-321-43447-1)** is available to adopting instructors. The Annotated Instructor's Edition is an exact replica of the student edition with the answers included.

Vocabulary Skills Study Card (Student / 0-321-31802-1)
Colorful, affordable, and packed with useful information, Longman's Vocabulary Study Card is a concise, 8-page reference guide to developing key vocabulary skills, such as learning to recognize context clues, reading a dictionary entry, and recognizing key root words, suffixes, and prefixes. Laminated for durability, students can keep this Study Card for years to come and pull it out whenever they need a quick review.

Oxford American College Dictionary (Student / 0-399-14415-3)
A hard cover reference with more than 175,000 entries.

The New American Webster Handy College Dictionary
(Student / 0-451-18166-2)
A paperback reference text with more than 100,000 entries.

MULTIMEDIA OFFERINGS

Interested in incorporating online materials into your course? Longman is happy to help. Our regional technology specialists provide training on all of our multimedia offerings.

MyReadingLab (www.myreadinglab.com)
This exciting new website houses all the media tools any developmental English student will need to improve their reading and study skills, and all in one easy-to-use place.

Other Books in This Series

Book 2: Effective Vocabulary (0-321-41071-8)
Book 3: Mastering Vocabulary (0-321-41072-6)

Acknowledgments

We are indebted to the many reviewers for their invaluable contributions. We would especially like to thank the following reviewers for their suggestions and guidance: Jennifer Britton, Valencia Community College; Dianne F. Kostelny, Okaloosa-Walton Community College; Lynn Campbell, Fresno City College; Lynda Wolverton, Polk Community College; Evelyn Koperwas, Broward Community College; Joyce Jacobs, Lee College; Wendy Wish, Valencia Community College; Bonnie Bailey, Arapahoe Community College; Carrie Pyhrr, Austin Community College; and Rebecca Suarez, University of Texas, El Paso.

Many people have helped make this project a gratifying journey. My campus colleague and good friend Mary Dubbé emboldened me to persevere. I thank her for balance, direction, and encouragement. My best virtual friend Janet Elder provided inspiration and levity in some of the most uncanny and well-timed communications. The connection is inexplicably delightful. For the art-work and photographs, I thank Molly Gamble-Walker, George Pongratz, and Elizabeth Pongratz. May their muses continue to provide. Finally, I am grateful for the patience, suggestions, and gracious attention from my editor Susan Kunchandy, who continues to give me courage in the quietest of ways.

—Susan Pongratz

It is such a thrill to partner with Susan Pongratz, a gifted teacher and writer, to provide this comprehensive vocabulary program. It is so gratifying to work with a kindred spirit who shares a deep devotion to students and clear vision for their academic success. In talent, creativity, and dedication, none can com-pare to Susan Pongratz, and I thank her for giving so much of herself. I would also like to thank Susan Kunchandy, Developmental Editor, and Melanie Craig, Acquisitions Editor, for their faith in our work. Finally, I would like to thank all of you who allow us to partner with you in your classroom instruction. It is an honor to be a part of your life's work!

—D. J. Henry

STUDY Tips

Throughout this book, you will be asked to practice using and working with new words. By creating study cards, you will enhance your in-depth knowledge of the words. Study the models to determine new ways of learning vocabulary.

Frayer Model

To complete a modified Frayer Model, follow these steps.
Write the word in the center of the card.

1. Definition/synonyms (one-word definitions) of the word.
2. Write characteristics or other forms of the word.
3. Write the antonyms.
4. Write a non-example.

Definition/Synonyms	Characteristics
Vocabulary Word	
Antonyms	Non-examples

Example 1

> **Synonyms**
> inspire, encourage, impel
>
> **Characteristics**
> excitement, cheering,
> eagerness to perform well
>
> ### motivate
>
> **Antonyms**
> depress, turn off, demotivate,
> stop, procrastinate
>
> **Non-examples**
> sunbathing, sleeping,
> putting things off until later,
> playing instead of practicing

Example 2

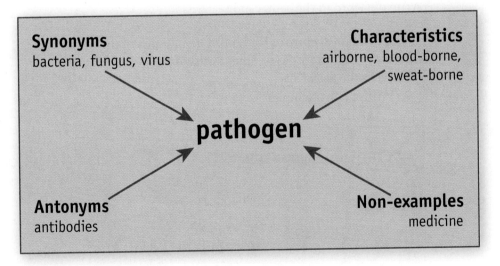

Synonyms
bacteria, fungus, virus

Characteristics
airborne, blood-borne,
sweat-borne

pathogen

Antonyms
antibodies

Non-examples
medicine

Visual Vocabulary Cards

Another way to learn new vocabulary words is to create cards with sketches or pictures to help you visualize the word and the definition. For example, to learn the word *ambivalent*, which means *having mixed emotions*, imagine being on a fence, not sure which side to choose. The image will help you connect the word and its meaning.

Example

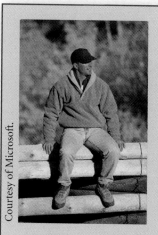

Courtesy of Microsoft.

Ambivalent

having mixed emotions; unsure; undecided

Ray was <u>ambivalent</u> about taking the new job; while he would make more money, it did not seem like interesting work.

Pyramid Summary

1. Write the vocabulary word.
2. List three synonyms (one-word definitions).
3. List the word parts and definitions (if available).
4. List antonyms (opposites) of the word.
5. Write a sentence using the word.

Supercilious

conceited, arrogant, prideful

Super- = above; cilium = eyelid; -ous = full of

Antonyms: humble, modest, warm, open, friendly, approachable

He had a supercilious attitude, looking down on everyone as if he owned them.

KIM

Divide the index card into three columns.

1. Write the vocabulary word in column 1.
2. Write any information you have about the word, such as the definition, synonyms, antonyms, and a sentence in column 2.
3. Create a drawing that represents the word in column 3.

Key Word	Information	Mental Image
Write the vocabulary word.	Write the definition, synonym, antonym, sentence.	Draw a picture.

Example

Zeal	**Definition:** Enthusiastic devotion to a cause **Synonyms:** passion, devotion, eagerness **Antonyms:** apathy, indifference **Sentence:** The new employee shows great <u>zeal</u> in working on the project.	

Using Context Clues and Word Analysis

Get Ready to Read About Context Clues and Word Analysis

A good vocabulary is one of the elements of academic success. Adding to your personal inventory of words is an ongoing process that requires knowledge of context clues and word parts. As you read through this chapter, consider your prior knowledge about the following words:

Vocabulary—the words used or understood by a person

Context clue—information that surrounds a new word and is used to understand its meaning

Synonym—a word that has the same or nearly the same meaning as another word

Antonym—a word that has the opposite meaning of another word

Prefix—a group of letters with a specific meaning that is added to the beginning of a word to form a new word

Root—the foundation of a word

Suffix—a group of letters with a specific meaning that is added to the end of a word to form a new meaning (Suffixes may also change the part of speech of a word.)

VOCABULARY IN CONTEXT

Developing an extensive personal collection of vocabulary words is an ongoing process. At the age of 4, you knew about 5,600 words. By the age of 10, you had acquired more than 34,000 words. By the time you are a college sophomore, you will know 120,000 words. Since words are symbols for ideas, you can see how important a good vocabulary is to understand and learn new concepts.

You can develop a strong vocabulary by reading a wide variety of material. Also, listen carefully to instructors, guest speakers, and other students. As you hear new words and observe people's use of words, you begin to understand the meanings of words. When you do this, you are considering the word in its context, or its surroundings. When you use **context clues**, you are examining the information that surrounds a new word used to understand its meaning.

—From "Vocabulary in Context" http://www.ucc.vt.edu/stdysk/vocabula.html retrieved 11/01/2005

The four most common types of context clues are:

- Synonyms
- Antonyms
- General context
- Examples

To remember these clues, a mnemonic device—that is, memory trick—is created by using the first letter of each clue to spell **SAGE**, which means *wise*. Learning to use context clues is a wise—or **sage**—reading strategy.

A **synonym** is a word that has the same or nearly the same meaning as another word. You can remember this because the prefix **syn-** means *same* and the root **nym** means *name*. For example, the words *funny* and *humorous* are synonyms since they both mean *amusing*. Clue words for identifying a synonym include *or* and *that is*.

An **antonym**, on the other hand, is a word that has the opposite meaning of another word. For example, *heavy* and *light* are antonyms. Antonyms present what a word is not. Look for contrast word clues such as *not, unlike, on the other hand, however, but, rather than, yet, unlike, in contrast*, and *as opposed to*.

A third way to determine the meaning of a new word requires that you rely on the **general context**. In other words, you will need to read the entire sentence, or even the next few sentences, to understand the meaning. In this case, you will find past experience, background knowledge, logic, and reasoning skills useful.

A final context clue is **example.** In this case, the author assumes you know something about the subject and will provide examples rather than a definition. Example signal words include *consisting of, for example, for instance, including, like,* and *such as.*

In addition to using context clues for vocabulary improvement, a skilled reader will study visual images and captions provided in textbooks. Likewise, a good reader will study graphs, charts, photographs, and cartoons.[*]

SAGE

Context Clue	Example	Definition
Synonym	The sports announcer said he would **segue**, or shift, to the sidelines for an interview with the coach.	To shift
Antonym	The tackle was a **pessimist**; on the other hand, the running back was always cheerful and hopeful for a win.	Someone with a negative outlook
General Context	Emily was **ecstatic** when she opened the Cracker Jack box and discovered a diamond engagement ring secretly placed there by her boyfriend.	Very happy
Example	Sometimes an author will use a **pseudonym**; for example, Samuel Clemens wrote under the name of Mark Twain and Stephen King has used the name Richard Bachman.	False name

[*] "Clues," by D. J. Henry from *The Skilled Reader,* pp. 45–57.

VISUAL VOCABULARY

Study the cartoon below and then choose the best definition based on the context.
Agnes by Tony Cochran November 01, 2005

Flaccid means ___b___.   a. fragrant.   b. flabby.   c. forceful.   d. noisy.

Copyright © 2005 Creators Syndicate, Inc. By permission of Tony Cochran and Creators Syndicate, Inc.
http://www.comics.com/creators/agnes/index.html

EXERCISE **1** Synonym Clues

A. Select the letter of the best definition for the word in **bold** print.

1. People who exercise and burn more calories than they consume will **accumulate**, or gain, less fat; therefore, they can lose weight slowly and effectively.

   ___b___ **Accumulate** means
   a. burn.   c. lose.
   b. gain.   d. exercise.

2. After a **vigorous** and lively practice with the track team, Brian still has time to do volunteer tutoring at the local Boys' and Girls' Club.

   ___a___ **Vigorous** means
   a. energetic.   c. exhausted.
   b. slow.   d. helpful.

3. Mr. Two-Feathers is such a good chess player that no one can predict his **strategy** until the plan is executed swiftly and suddenly he has won the game.

   ___c___ **Strategy** means
   a. game.   c. plan.
   b. swift blow.   d. message.

4. The fire chaplain received a special **commendation** from the firefighters who wanted to show their appreciation for her outstanding courage and compassion.

_____c_____ **Commendation** means

    a. decision.   c. award.

    b. courage.   d. publicity.

5. Because the stock seemed to **fluctuate**—that is, move up and down—our financial advisor recommended that we sell and invest in real estate instead.

_____a_____ **Fluctuate** means

    a. vary.   c. decrease.

    b. increase.   d. remain constant.

B. Fill in the blank with the meaning of the word in **bold** print.

6. Often, the two things that **hinder**, or prevent, good reading comprehension and a faster reading rate are a lack of background knowledge about the topic and a limited vocabulary.

Hinder means _to prevent or hold back_.

7. The candidate for mayor had a reputation for being **deceitful** and untrustworthy, so the voters elected his opponent.

Deceitful means _dishonest_.

8. As penalty for her thoughtless prank, the judge gave the young woman 400 hours of community service and three years of probation, after which time, the offense could be **expunged**, or removed, from her record.

Expunge means _remove_.

9. **Ingestion** (intake) of a mold on rye flour, which caused hallucinations, is one theory about what caused the Salem witch trials.

Ingestion means _eating, drinking, or intake_.

10. Some teens who recently experimented with eating jimson weed—a **toxic**, or poisonous, plant that often grows on the side of the road—became violently ill with a life-threatening condition.

Toxic means _poisonous_.

EXERCISE 2 Antonym Clues

A. Select the letter of the best definition for the word in **bold** print.

1. After reading the assigned book, researching for several days, and writing numerous drafts until he finally turned in an excellent essay, Jess remarked, "It feels good to do a project with **integrity** rather than cutting corners and completing it dishonestly."

  _c_ **Integrity** means
  a. hardship.   c. honesty.
  b. difficulty.   d. dishonesty.

2. Because they are gradually becoming the **prey** instead of the hunters, lions are less numerous and may someday face extinction if they are not protected.

  _a_ **Prey** means
  a. target.   c. traveler.
  b. hunter.   d. wanderer.

3. The year was filled with some **calamities,** but we also had some joyous occasions marked by good fortune.

  _b_ **Calamity** means
  a. joy.   c. confusion.
  b. tragedy.   d. blessing.

4. Although our physics professor's lectures are well organized and very clear, the departmental tests are **vague** and confusing.

  _d_ **Vague** means
  a. clear.   c. recognized.
  b. well organized.   d. unclear.

5. Unlike the superheroes who are always viewed with great respect, literature's famous **villains** are usually disliked, even when there is a good explanation for their bad behavior.

  _a_ **Villain** means
  a. evil person.   c. sidekick.
  b. hero.   d. champion.

B. Fill in the blank with the meaning of the word in **bold** print.

6. Striving to be **mediocre** requires little effort, but striving for excellence requires hard work and the faith to aim high.

Mediocre means _unexceptional or average with no effort_ .

7. The power of a phrase such as "I love you" can **diminish** if it is used too often without truth, but it can expand if it is used sparingly and with earnest feeling.

Diminish means <u>lessen in value or meaning</u>.

8. Although they had been **rivals** for many years, the two businessmen eventually became friends and formed a corporation of the two companies, proving that becoming allies was more profitable than competing.

Rival means <u>competitor or enemy</u>.

9. Introverts tend to be shy and reflective, and therefore need some private thinking time in **isolation**; however, most also appreciate some opportunities to mix socially.

Isolation means <u>aloneness or separation or privacy</u>.

10. A **minimal** procedure, noninvasive surgery is becoming more popular than older kinds of surgery that require complex procedures and long hospital stays.

Minimal means <u>slightest or least possible</u>.

EXERCISE **3** General Context Clues

A. Select the letter of the best definition for the word in **bold** print.

1. To **lure** recent graduates to join their corporation, recruiters interview seniors and often use dinners, free trips, and other attractive perks as encouragement.

<u> d </u> **Lure** means
a. work.   c. graduate.
b. study.   d. attract.

2. The **epitome** of a great leader is someone who has vision, humility, confidence, and good communication skills.

<u> a </u> **Epitome** means
a. perfect model.   c. ability.
b. skill.   d. training.

3. Computers, coffee shops, and fast food restaurants are more **ubiquitous** now than they were fifty years ago.

<u> b </u> **Ubiquitous** means
a. expensive.   c. rare.
b. ever-present.   d. disappointing.

4. We sailed a few miles into the gulf and then dropped anchor near a distant **cay**, which we waded out to so we could explore its beach and island plants.

   __a__ **Cay** means
   - a. coral island.
   - b. island restaurant.
   - c. buried treasure.
   - d. old sailing vessel.

5. In order to **orient** yourself to college life, you should make connections during your freshman seminar; learn to use resources such as the computer center and the library; and locate the offices that provide financial aid, student activities, technical support, and career information.

   __d__ **Orient** means
   - a. associate without interest.
   - b. examine.
   - c. determine with difficulty.
   - d. become familiar with.

B. Fill in the blank with the meaning of the word in **bold** print.

6. After we decided to **modify** our plans for the steel bridge contest, we were sure we would win because the design was better than last year's entry.

   Modify means _change_ .

7. Many successful people make their dreams a reality because of their ability to **persevere** and stick with a plan, rather than give up at the first sign of disappointment.

   Persevere means _to continue in a determined way_ .

8. Some college classes are purely lecture courses in which the professor provides information to the students, and other classes are taught as seminars in which students also share their own **contemplations** about their readings and research.

   Contemplation means _thoughts_ .

9. One of the best things college students can do to make connections and avoid a feeling of **alienation** is to get involved in a campus activity.

   Alienation means _isolation or separation_ .

10. Before they can register for electives or courses in their major, most freshmen must take the **obligatory** core courses to ensure they have a foundation of knowledge for the next classes.

    Obligatory means _mandatory or required_ .

EXERCISE 🟦 Example Clues

A. Select the letter of the best definition for the word in **bold** print.

1. Cheryl was so confident, beautiful, and thoughtless that she seemed **oblivious** to the way she hurt other people's feelings with cruel comments, unkind observations, or heartless stares.

   ___d___ **Oblivious** means

   a. honest.   c. untidy.
   b. united.   d. unaware.

2. The **disparaging** remarks such as "Why isn't this essay an A?" or "What did the other students get on the project?" or "Can't you do any better than this on a calculus exam?" discouraged Adam, even though he excelled in almost everything he tried.

   ___a___ **Disparaging** means

   a. critical; negative.   c. interesting; observant.
   b. encouraging; positive.   d. boring; negative.

3. The factory workers agreed to show their **solidarity** against the new company policies in a number of ways; for example, they walked out of the building arm-in-arm, chanting their displeasure, and refused to sign the new contract.

   ___a___ **Solidarity** means

   a. unity.   c. suggestion.
   b. pleasure.   d. comfort.

4. Because of a weak stomach, Matt often suffered from **queasiness** whenever he rode a roller coaster, sat in the back seat of a car, traveled by airplane, or even looked over the ledge when we were hiking in the mountains.

   ___b___ **Queasiness** means

   a. excitement.   c. arrangement.
   b. uneasiness.   d. order.

5. My co-worker often gives **pathetic** excuses for missing work such as "I fell asleep in the shower" or "My radio station started playing Christmas carols, so I thought I was on vacation when the alarm went off."

   ___d___ **Pathetic** means

   a. strong; believable.   c. important; impressive.
   b. honorable; praiseworthy.   d. pitiful; weak.

B. Fill in the blank with the meaning of the word in **bold** print.

6. A **recurrence** of things such as a nightmare that revisits every night, or an unexplained feeling of dread, can put a person on edge and cause feelings of anxiety.

Recurrence means <u>return; something happening again and again</u>.

7. Since the breakup with her boyfriend, Ruth Ann **broods** by wandering campus alone and staying locked in her room for hours at a time.

Brood means <u>to be gloomy</u>.

8. When Alex was a child, he tried to **emulate** heroes such as his father, his soccer coach, his youth minister, and his favorite football player.

Emulate means <u>copy or model after</u>.

9. To prove how much he **cherished** his wife, Ted started helping with the housework, cooking meals several times a week, and volunteering to pick up groceries on the way home from work.

Cherish means <u>love</u>.

10. As a new employee, Phil was **reluctant** to take on new roles such as project leader because he still did not know office policies or state standards.

Reluctant means <u>unwilling</u>.

EXERCISE 5 Vocabulary in Context

A. Select the letter of the best definition for the word in **bold** print.

1. When psychologists study birth order, they often notice similar personality traits between only children and first-born children who have younger **siblings.**

<u>c</u>   **Sibling** means
   a. parents.   c. brother or sister.
   b. relatives.   d. close friends.

2. Because broken objects can provide interest to a photograph, Raoul likes to pose his fashion models in front of **deteriorating** barns and abandoned houses.

<u>a</u>   **Deteriorating** means
   a. falling apart.   c. new.
   b. strengthening.   d. improving.

3. Students who work with **diligence** find their success leads to more success if they work carefully and thoroughly.

___b___ **Diligence** means

    a. humor.   c. carelessness.

    b. careful work.   d. distraction.

4. At seafood festivals, we tend to **gravitate** toward the aroma of fried hush-puppies, crab cakes, oysters, clams, and funnel cake.

___c___ **Gravitate** means

    a. avoid.   c. drift.

    b. ignore.   d. left.

5. Whenever I **embark** on a new adventure, I feel a sense of excitement about the change as well as a fear of the unknown and a hope that something better lies ahead.

___a___ **Embark** means

    a. start out.   c. drift.

    b. end.   d. understand.

B. Fill in the blank with the meaning of the word in **bold** print.

6. Everyone would rather listen to a speaker who believes **ardently** in a cause than someone who is indifferent and has no passion.

Ardently means _enthusiastically_____.

7. **Advocates** of early childhood education are urging parents to talk frequently to their children to help promote reading readiness, language skills, and cognitive development.

Advocate means _supporter_____.

8. Steven Spielberg once said, "We have **exalted** the image at the expense of the written word," which means that we love movies more than books—something that concerned the famous filmmaker.

Exalt means _praise_____.

9. John's grandmother taught him to ignore **trivial** things such as a flat tire, slow-moving traffic, or running out of milk, because those unimportant events can prevent us from seeing the beauty and joy in the big picture of life.

Trivial means _minor or petty_____.

10. If we have not been taught good manners or proper etiquette, we may **unwittingly** offend someone by using the wrong fork or hovering around the banquet table instead of mingling and making polite conversation.

Unwitting means <u>unaware</u>   .

Word Analysis

Concepts, or ideas, are made up of words, and words are made up of smaller parts. By studying word parts, you can determine the definitions of new words, memorize meanings more effectively, and improve your spelling ability. In fact, the word *misspell* is a combination of the prefix *mis-*, which means *wrong*, and the root *spell*. Thus, because a single word part can appear in hundreds of words, learning some Greek and Latin **prefixes, roots**, and **suffixes** can help you unlock the meanings of many more words and act as a spelling aid as you write.

Study the chart below to see the role word parts play in vocabulary development by considering the parts of the word *inspector*.

Root	Foundation of the word	spect	"look"
Prefix	Found at the beginning of a word	in-	"into"
Suffix	Found at the end of a word	-or	"one who"

Roots

The roots of words form the foundation. Many of our word roots are taken from Latin and Greek. Learning to recognize roots will help you understand the meanings of many new words.

EXAMPLE Write the root and meanings of the following words: acrophobia, arachnophobia, photophobia, claustrophobia, phobic.

Phob means *fear; acrophobia* is a fear of heights; *arachnophobia* is a fear of spiders, or arachnids; *photophobia* is a fear (or sensitivity) to light; *claustrophobia* is a fear of closed-in places; and *phobic* is an adjective that means *characteristic of having an excessive fear.*

EXPLANATION Each of the words has the root *phob* in common. By adding a prefix, another root, or a suffix to the foundation, new words are formed.

EXERCISE **1** Root Words

Study the following words and their definitions to determine the definition of each root.

1. empathy: an understanding of another's feelings or situation
   apathy: a lack of concern or interest
   sympathy: the act of sharing the feelings of another

   __b__ *Path* means
   - a. situation.
   - b. feeling.
   - c. interest.
   - d. sharing.

2. forcible: characterized by strength
   enforce: to compel obedience
   fortify: to make strong

   __a__ *Forc, fort* mean
   - a. strong.
   - b. united.
   - c. compel.
   - d. cause.

3. generation: offspring from the same level of descent from a common ancestor
   regenerate: to give new life or form
   degenerate: to decline from an original form

   __d__ *Gen* means
   - a. destruction.
   - b. observation.
   - c. level.
   - d. origin.

4. sequence: a following of one thing after another
   consequence: result
   subsequent: next

   __c__ *Seque* means
   - a. show concern.
   - b. arrange.
   - c. follow.
   - d. find.

5. biology: science of life processes of plants and animals
   microbiology: study of life processes of small organisms
   biography: history of individual lives

   __c__ *Bio* means
   - a. science.
   - b. study.
   - c. life.
   - d. history.

6. autobiography: story of one's own life written or dictated by that person
autograph: a person's own signature
graphology: study of handwriting

___d___ *Graph* means
    a. life.   c. story.
    b. person.   d. write.

7. solitude: lonely or isolated place; state of being alone
soliloquy: act of talking to one's self
solace: comfort; an easing of grief, sorrow, or loneliness

___a___ *Sol* means
    a. alone.   c. talking.
    b. place.   d. grief.

8. neonatal: having to do with a newborn
neophyte: beginner
neologism: new meaning for a word

___b___ *Neo* means
    a. word.   c. last.
    b. new.   d. simple.

9. lithograph: a design created from a flat surface of stone or metal that repels ink
lithosphere: the rocky part of the earth's crust
lithoid: stonelike

___c___ *Lith* means
    a. surface.   c. stone.
    b. metal.   d. ink.

10. magnanimous: generous; big hearted; noble
magnify: to enlarge
magnate: a very important, powerful, or important person in his or her field

___a___ *Magna, magni* mean
    a. large.   c. size.
    b. weak.   d. small.

EXERCISE 🔢 Root Words

Study the chart below and insert a second example of a word that contains each root. (Answers may vary.)

Root Words Guide

Root	Definition	Example	Example
aqua	water	aquamarine	_____
bene	good	benefit	_____
bio	life	biology	_____
cap	head	capitalize	_____
dent	tooth	dentition	_____
derm	skin	epidermis	_____
duc, duct	lead, guide	conductor	_____
ego	self	egotistical	_____
equ, equal	equal	inequity	_____
err, errat	wander	erratic	_____
flu, fluct, flux	flow	reflux	_____
graph	write, draw	biography	_____
ject	throw	trajectory	_____
loc	place	locomotion	_____
log	speech, science, reason	monolog	_____
miss, mit	send, let go	emit	_____
mot, mov	movement	motive	_____
mut, muta	change	mutation	_____
pater	father	paternal	_____
path	suffering, feeling	apathy	_____
phobia	fear	acrophobia	_____
phon	sound	phonetic	_____
port	carry	transport	_____
pon, pos, posit	put, place	imposition	_____
psych	mind	psychology	_____

Root	Definition	Example	Example
quir	ask	query	_____
scope	see	telescope	_____
sect	cut	dissect	_____
seque	follow	subsequent	_____
soro	sister	sorority	_____
struct	build	construction	_____
tact	touch	tactile	_____
tain, tent	hold	maintain	_____
therma	heat	thermometer	_____
tract	drag, pull	intractable	_____
vis	see	revise	_____

Prefixes

A prefix appears at the beginning of a word and changes the meaning of a word. In fact, *pre-* means *before.* For instance, consider the word *kind,* which means *gentle* and *caring.* If you add the prefix *un-*, however, you negate the word, or change its meaning to a negative word, which means *not gentle* or *not caring.* If you arrange prefixes into categories, it is easier to remember them. Look at the examples below.

Negative	Placement	Numbers	Time
un- (not)	*ab-* (away)	*uni-* (one)	*pre-* (before)
il- (not)	*circum-* (around)	*bi-* (two)	*post-* (after)
anti- (against)	*trans-* (across)	*tri-* (three)	*re-* (again)
mis- (wrong)	*inter-* (between)	*cent-* (hundred)	*retro-* (back)

EXAMPLE We took a **pretest** at the beginning of the semester, and then, before our final exam, we took a **posttest** to determine how much our skills had improved.

Pretest means: <u>a test taken before the information is presented to determine your</u> <u>prior knowledge.</u>

Posttest means: <u>a test taken after the information is presented to see how much you</u> <u>have learned.</u>

EXPLANATION   Since the prefix *pre-* means *before*, a pretest determines how much a student knows *before* a lesson is taught. On the other hand, the prefix *post-* means *after*, and a posttest is administered *after* a lesson to assess what information the student has gained. Instructors compare the before and after scores to determine their students' progress.

EXERCISE 1 Prefixes

Study the following words and their definitions to determine the definition of each prefix.

1. atypical: not normal
   amoral: without principles
   apolitical: not interested in politics

   ___c___ *A-* means
   - a. many.
   - b. for.
   - c. not; without.
   - d. from; outside.

2. absent: not present
   abate: to lessen
   absolve: to take away guilt; pardon

   ___a___ *Ab-* means
   - a. away, from.
   - b. above.
   - c. alone.
   - d. within.

3. antidote: a remedy used against a poison
   antiwar: opposed to fighting
   antagonist: an enemy; opponent

   ___b___ *Anti-* means
   - a. around.
   - b. against.
   - c. between.
   - d. before.

4. autobiography: story about one's life written or dictated by that person
   autograph: a person's signature
   autonomy: independence

   ___a___ *Auto-* means
   - a. self.
   - b. one.
   - c. many.
   - d. alone.

5. circumference: distance around
circumvent: avoid
circumspect: cautious

_____b_____ *Circum-* means

a. between.   c. under.
b. around.   d. above.

6. commence: begin
comprise: to make up; include
commemorate: honor; remember with others

_____c_____ *Com-* means

a. between.   c. with; together.
b. during.   d. down; away.

7. descend: to lower
detract: to take away from
delete: to get rid of

_____c_____ *De-* means

a. above; more than normal.   c. from; down; away.
b. between.   d. during.

8. divulge: to tell
dilemma: a hard choice
diversion: a pastime one enjoys after working

_____d_____ *Di-* means

a. question.   c. many.
b. play.   d. two.

9. disaster: a tragedy
dissect: to separate parts for further study
dispatch: to send

_____d_____ *Dis-* means

a. in; within.   c. between; during.
b. around.   d. not; separated from.

10. enhance: improve
enliven: make lively or spirited
enchant: cast a spell; bewitch; charm

_____d_____ *En-* means

a. outside.   c. down.
b. around.   d. within.

EXERCISE 2 Prefixes

Study the chart below and insert a second example of a word that contains each prefix. (Answers will vary.)

Prefixes Guide

Prefix	Definition	Example	Example
a-	not, without	apolitical	_____
ab-	away, from	absent	_____
auto-	self	autonomy	_____
con-	with, together	constitute	_____
dis-	not, separated from	disinterest	_____
e-	out, from	evolve	_____
ex-	out, from	expel	_____
hyper-	above, excessive	hypertension	_____
hypo-	below, under	hypotension	_____
in-	not	incomprehensible	_____
im-	not	imperfect	_____
micro-	small	microscopic	_____
per-	through	perimeter	_____
re-	again	replay	_____
retro-	backward	retroactive	_____
sub-	under, below	submarine	_____
super-	above, over, beyond	supervisor	_____
sym-	together, with	symmetry	_____
tele-	far, from a distance	televise	_____

Suffixes

A suffix appears at the end of a word and changes the meaning of a word as well as its part of speech. For instance, the base word *mother* (a noun or a verb) can be changed slightly by adding the suffix *-ly* to create the word *motherly* (adjective) or *–hood* to create the word *motherhood* (noun).

EXAMPLE   The word *credible*, which means *believable*, comes from the root *cred* (believe) added to the suffix *-ible* (able to). However, using the same root *cred*, you can also make 12 more words. Use your dictionary to identify the parts of speech and definitions of the following words.

1. credentials: (n.) proof of authority

2. credence: (n.) acceptance as true

3. credit: (n.) reliance on truth; (v.) to trust in the truth of

4. creditability: (n.) worthiness of belief

5. creditable: (adj.) worthy of belief

6. creditableness: (n.) worthiness of commercial credit

7. creditably: (adv.) done in a manner worthy of commercial credit

8. credibility: (n.) the quality of inspiring belief

9. credo: (n.) a statement of personal belief

10. credulity: (n.) readiness to believe

11. credulous: (adj.) ready to believe

12. credulously: (adv.) in a believing manner

EXPLANATION   Suffixes such as *-ity* and *-ence* have specific meanings and usually indicate nouns; likewise for *-able* and *-ous*, which usually indicate adjectives and *-ly* which often indicates an adverb.

EXERCISE 1 Suffixes

Study the following words and their definitions to determine the definition of each suffix.

1. reusable: capable of being used again
   notable: worthy of mention
   programmable: able to be systematically planned

   ___b___ *-Able* means
   a. away; from.   c. with; together.
   b. capable of.   d. above; excessive.

2. remembrance: the state of being remembered
acquaintance: a relationship less intimate than friendship
abundance: a great amount

_____a_____ -*Ance* means
    a. state of.
    b. one who.
    c. belief.
    d. specialist.

3. education: the act of obtaining knowledge or skill
notation: system of using figures, symbols, or words
commendation: praise

_____a_____ -*Ation* means
    a. action; process.
    b. state of.
    c. quality.
    d. one who.

4. investigate: examine
isolate: set apart
alienate: turn away

_____c_____ -*Ate* means
    a. direction.
    b. in a certain manner.
    c. cause to become.
    d. state; quality.

5. fratricide: killing of one's brother or sister
genocide: extermination of a national, ethnic, religious, or political group
homicide: killing of one person by another

_____c_____ -*Cide* means
    a. brother.
    b. politics.
    c. kill.
    d. crime.

6. teacher: a person who is hired to instruct
leader: a person who provides direction
presenter: one who offers demonstrations

_____d_____ -*Er* means
    a. teach.
    b. direction.
    c. state or condition.
    d. one who.

7. simplify: make less complicated
electrify: thrill or startle greatly
solidify: make solid

_____b_____ -*Fy* means
    a. quality or state.
    b. cause to become.
    c. in the direction of.
    d. in a certain manner.

8. bountiful: plenty
beautiful: attractive, handsome
fearful: frightening

___c___ -*Ful* means

    a. one who.
    b. state.

    c. full of.
    d. quality.

9. motherhood: state of being a mother
parenthood: state of being a parent
sisterhood: state of being a sister

___a___ -*Hood* means

    a. state of.
    b. in a certain manner.

    c. full of.
    d. one who.

10. feverish: burning
childish: like a child
foolish: arousing laughter

___d___ -*Ish* means

    a. full of.
    b. in the direction of.

    c. quality; degree.
    d. like; related to.

EXERCISE 2 Suffixes

Study the chart below and insert a second example of a word that contains each suffix and then its part of speech.

Suffixes Guide

Suffix	Definition	Example	Example	Part of Speech
-acle	quality, state	spectacle	_____	noun
-al	of, like, related to, being	focal	_____	adjective
-ator	one who	spectator	_____	noun
-ation	action, process	imitation	_____	noun
-er	person, doer	teacher	_____	noun
-ful	full of	beautiful	_____	adjective
-ible	capable of	compatible	_____	adjective
-ic	of, like, related to, being	toxic	_____	adjective

Suffix	Definition	Example	Example	Part of Speech
-ical	of, like, related to, being	stoical	_____	adjective
-ician	specialist	technician	_____	noun
-ify	cause to become	glorify	_____	verb
-ile	of, like, related to, being	infantile	_____	adjective
-ist	person	chemist	_____	noun
-ition	action, process	nutrition	_____	noun
-ity	quality, trait	quantity	_____	noun
-ive	of, like, related to, being	sensitive	_____	adjective
-ize	cause to become	tantalize	_____	verb
-ly	in a certain manner	slowly	_____	adverb
-ology	science, study of	microbiology	_____	noun
-or	person, doer	author	_____	noun
-ous	full of, like	loquacious	_____	adjective
-y	quality, trait	showy	_____	adjective

Analogies

Analogies are word relationships that require critical thinking. The pairs of words are like puzzles that require the reader to determine the relationship presented. For example, daughter : girl :: son : boy. You would read this analogy as, "Daughter is to girl as son is to boy." Note that the first step is to make sure you know the definitions of all of the words. Next, you determine the relationship presented.

Analogies can present several kinds of relationships.

- Synonym (kind : nice :: unfriendly : mean).
- Antonym (friendly : mean :: heavy : light).
- A descriptive relationship (strong : wrestler :: tall : skyscraper).
- The relationship of the part to a whole (leg : body :: tire : car).
- The relationship of an item to a category (cabin : dwelling :: painting : art).

EXERCISE 1 Synonyms and Antonyms

Step 1: Determine the definitions and part of speech of each of the pairs.
Step 2: Determine the relationship of the first pair.
Step 3: Select the letter of the answer that completes the second pair with the same relationship as the first pair.

1. employee : bonus :: player : __a__
   a. trophy   b. runner   c. opponent

2. fortify : weaken :: simplify : __c__
   a. clean   b. discuss   c. complicate

3. accumulate : gather :: tutor : __c__
   a. send   b. mail   c. teach

4. hinder : prevent :: walk : __c__
   a. end   b. find   c. hike

5. toxic : poisonous :: circular : __a__
   a. round   b. similar   c. excited

6. villain : hero :: fragrant : __a__
   a. odorous   b. quick   c. talented

7. prey : hunter :: suspect : __b__
   a. sport   b. detective   c. passenger

8. vague : clear :: heavy : __a__
   a. light   b. sincere   c. difficult

9. reluctant : eager :: open : __c__
   a. dazzling   b. bold   c. closed

10. mediocre : excellent :: straight : __c__
    a. plump   b. narrow   c. crooked

EXERCISE 2 Descriptive, Part to Whole, Item to Category

1. storm : cyclone :: celebration : __a__
   a. Cinco de Mayo   b. exam   c. courtroom

2. assets : savings account :: fleet : __a__
   a. aircraft carrier   b. termination   c. admiral

3. fluctuate : temperatures :: rise : __c__
   a. medicines   b. prescription   c. helium balloons

4. ruler : monarch :: elected official : __b__
   a. grocer   b. president   c. receptionist

5. nonfiction : biography :: building : __c__
   a. beverage   b. floor   c. cabin

6. empire: magnate :: company : __a__
   a. chief executive officer   b. assistant   c. file clerk

7. biology : microbiology :: engineering : __c__
   a. art   b. photography   c. civil engineering

8. pill : placebo :: signature : __b__
   a. money   b. forgery   c. insurance

9. assessment : pretest :: student : __c__
   a. lawyer   b. carpenter   c. freshman

10. anecdote : speech :: spice : __a__
   a. meal   b. gold   c. technology

Stop and Think

Read the following passage and use context clues to select the best word to fill the blank.

Today, **(1)** students_____ of all ages fill college classrooms. In fact, 28 is the average age of a current community college student. Many of these students are returning to the **(2)** classroom_____ after years on the job and away from the books. Returning students often face many stresses. The first **(3)** problem_____ many face is the college system. Dealing with admissions and financial aid, transferring **(4)** credits_____, and registering for classes can be an overwhelming process. Once classes begin, these students often find balancing classwork, family **(5)** life_____, and jobs challenging and tiring. Finally, many of these older students feel the **(6)** pressure_____ to keep up with other college students. Despite these challenges, returning students are often the most successful students in their **(7)** classes_____.

1. a. students   b. conditions
2. a. mall   b. classroom
3. a. story   b. problem
4. a. credits   b. patients
5. a. life   b. presents
6. a. pressure   b. wish
7. a. rooms   b. classes

 Visit the following Websites for more practice with context clues and word parts.

http://wps.ablongman.com/long_licklider_vocabulary_1/ 0,1682,11668-,00.html

http://wps.ablongman.com/long_licklider_vocabulary_1/ 0,1682,11839-,00.html

CHAPTER

2 Dictionary Skills

Get Ready to Read About Dictionary Skills

A good collegiate dictionary is an important tool for a skilled reader. Learning to use all of the features of the dictionary will also improve your speaking and writing skills. As you prepare to read this chapter, think about what you know about the type of information a dictionary provides. Also, think about what you know about other reference materials such as a thesaurus and a textbook glossary.

> *Polonius:* What do you read, my lord?
> *Hamlet:* Words, words, words.
> *Polonius:* What is the matter, my lord?
> *Hamlet:* Between who?
> *Polonius:* I mean, the matter that you read, my lord.

William Shakespeare, *Hamlet*, II, ii

Words! They fascinate, energize, inspire, defeat, discourage, and immortalize. Using the right word can make an impact on your listeners. College is a great place to develop effective communication skills through vocabulary development.

Comedian Steven Wright once said, "I was reading the dictionary. I thought it was a poem about everything." A dictionary contains a great deal of information; knowing how to use it correctly can enhance the quality of both your life and your education. Learning to use a dictionary as a tool to develop your vocabulary can also improve your reading comprehension and reading speed. In addition, it can improve your written and oral communication.

Looking at the selection from *Hamlet* by William Shakespeare, you can see how a word can have several meanings, and how choosing the right word is important in writing and speaking. In addition to providing definitions and multiple meanings of words, dictionaries include the pronunciation, the etymology (history), the part of speech, and special uses of words.

Linguists (people who study language) consider the origins of words as well as how language has evolved because our language is dynamic—it changes. Therefore, a current collegiate dictionary is an essential tool for every college student.

Consider the following features of most dictionaries:

- Guide Words (the words at the top of each page)
- Spelling (how the word and its different forms are spelled)
- Syllabication (the word divided into syllables)
- Pronunciation (how to say the word)
- Part of speech (the type of word)
- Definition (the meaning of the word, with the most common meaning listed first)
- Synonyms (words that have similar meaning)
- Etymology (the history of the word)

How to Find and Read Word Entries in the Dictionary

Guide Words

Take a look at your phone book. On the top of each page is a letter and then the parts of two names to help you determine which page you need to use as a reference. For example, to find the phone number for Edward Germain, you would look on the page with the following guide words:

Gen-Ges

Guide words in the dictionary help you find a given word in the same manner. Instead of reading the entire page, you can refer to the pair of words at the top of each page. These words indicate the first and last word, so by considering the alphabetical order, you can determine which page to use for your word search. This tool will help you increase your efficiency when using the dictionary. For example, if you want to find the word *emotional*, you would look on the page with the following heading:

408 emissary • employment

EXAMPLE Select the page and guide words you would use to look for the word *music*.

a. 782 metonym • mettle   c. 818 murk • music hall
b. 797 mnemonic • mode   d. 819 musician • mutably

EXPLANATION The answer is c. Alphabetically, *music* will fall between *murk* and *music hall*.

Spelling and Syllables

In a dictionary entry, the spelling of the word is first given in bold type. In addition, the word is divided into syllables. A syllable is a unit of sound, and it includes one vowel sound. For instance, the word *read* has two vowels, *e* and *a*, but only one vowel sound, which is a long *e*.

In words with more than one syllable, the stress marks that indicate the syllables that are emphasized will guide you in the proper pronunciation of the word. *Note:* Often, adding a suffix can change the stress and thus the pronunciation of a word.

EXAMPLE *compare* (kəm-pâr′) *comparable* (kŏm′pər-ə-bəl)

EXPLANATION *Compare* has two syllables. The second syllable is stressed more than the first, which is apparent because of the primary stress mark after the letter *r*. Now note how the stress mark changes for the word *comparable*, which has four syllables. The first syllable is now the one that is stressed more than the other three syllables. As you can see, learning to read the symbols in a dictionary entry will help you communicate more effectively, and noting the stress marks is critical to pronouncing words correctly. For this reason, dictionaries contain a pronunciation key.

Pronunciation Symbols

Study the chart below to learn how to interpret other symbols when using a dictionary for pronunciation.

Syllable	A unit of sound that includes at least one vowel sound.
Brève ⌣	This indicates a short vowel sound: ă = mat ŏ = hot ĕ = den ŭ = cup ĭ = sit
Macron —	This indicates a long vowel sound, which "says" the name of the letter. For example: ā (dā = day) ē (sē = see) ī (hīd = hide) ō (grō = grow) yo͞o (kyo͞ot = cute)
Schwa ə	This indicates the vowel sound of an unaccented syllable and is always pronounced "uh." ago item festival famous gypsum ə-gō′ ī′-təm fĕs′-tə-v'l fā′-məs jĭp′-səm

EXERCISE 1 Phonetic Spelling

Select the letter of the correct phonetic spelling for the word in **bold** print.

__a__   **1.** We often think **of** you during the holidays.
　　a. ŭv　　　　　　　　b. öf

__b__   **2.** We always **read** for at least fifteen minutes every day.
　　a. rĕd　　　　　　　　b. rēd

__b__   **3.** Today I **wrote** my boyfriend a letter.
　　a. rŏt　　　　　　　　b. rōt

__b__   **4.** I'm looking for a good interest **rate** on certificates of deposit.
　　a. răt　　　　　　　　b. rāt

__b__   **5.** Since Molly's foot is so slender, she always has difficulty finding a good **fit.**
　　a. fīt　　　　　　　　b. fĭt

_____a_____ **6.** I lost my balance when I had one foot on the pier and one in the
boat.
a. bōt   b. bŏt

_____b_____ **7.** Before we could purchase a car, we had to apply for a loan at the
credit **union.**
a. ŭ′nyən   b. yo͞on′yən

_____a_____ **8.** We decided to take a vacation on the West **Coast** this year.
a. kōst   b. kŏst

_____a_____ **9.** Instead of driving to Texas, we took a **plane.**
a. plān   b. plăn

_____a_____ **10.** My **one** wish for you is that you find your niche in life.
a. wŭn   b. ŏn

Study the dictionary entry below.

¹**home** \'hōm\ *n* [ME *hom,* fr OE *hām* village, home; akin to OHG *heim* home, Lith
šeima family, servants, Skt *ḳsema* habitable, *ḳseti* he dwells Gk *ktisein* to inhabit]
(bef 12c) **1a:** one's place of residence : DOMICILE **b:** HOUSE **2:** the social unit
formed by a family living together **3a** : a familiar or usual setting : congenial
environment; also : the focus of one's domestic attention <~is where the heart
is> **b:** HABITAT **4a** : a place of origin <salmon returning to their ~ to spawn>;
also : one's own country <having troubles at ~ and abroad> **b:** HEADQUARTERS 2
<~ of the dance company> **5** : an establishment providing residence and care for
people with special needs <~ for the elderly> **6** : the objective in various games;
esp : HOME PLATE

Source: By permission from *Merriam-Webster's Collegiate Dictionary,* 11th edition ©2005 by Merriam-Webster,
Incorporated (www.Merriam-Webster.com).

Definitions

Dictionary entries usually have more than one meaning, so the definitions will
be numbered, followed by the part of speech. The definition will sometimes be
accompanied by a sentence of explanation of usage to clarify each meaning.

Multiple Meanings and Context Clues

To determine which of the multiple meanings you should use, apply what you
have learned about context clues. Knowing how to recognize the parts of
speech will also be a guide to the appropriate definition.

EXAMPLE Study the dictionary excerpt for *home,* then select the number of the definition that best fits its use in the sentences below.

___1a___ **1.** We ran home before the rain started.

___6___ **2.** When Josh hit the ball out of the ballpark, his coach yelled, "Run home! Run home!"

___4b___ **3.** Although he is based in the home office in San Diego, Alex travels worldwide for his company.

EXPLANATION Each correct definition is coupled with a synonym to guide the reader. In sentence 1, *home* means *domicile*; in sentence 2, it means *home plate*; and in sentence 3, it means *headquarters*.

Connotation and Denotation

To communicate effectively, you will recognize that many words have a denotation as well as a connotation. **Denotation** means the dictionary definition. **Connotation** means the implied, or suggested, meaning. Furthermore, some words may have a positive connotation or a negative connotation. For example, one definition for *house* says, "A building that serves as a living quarters for one or more families." Although the word *home* also has a similar first definition— "one's place of residence"—it implies a place of safety, memories, warmth, and love—much more than just a dwelling.

Marketing strategies often involve recognizing the power of language. For example, because of the positive connotation of *home,* you would use that term rather than *house* if you were a realtor. Likewise, as a car salesman, you would sell *pre-owned* cars rather than *used* cars, because the word *used* negatively suggests something worn out, while the word *pre-owned* implies the car received great care from the previous owner.

EXAMPLE Check the statement below that has a positive connotation (sounds more compassionate).

___✓___ His father passed last week.

_____ His father died last week.

_____ His father kicked the bucket last week.

EXPLANATION Although you would not say anything as negative as "His father kicked the bucket," many people prefer *passed* because it suggests the loved one has moved to a better place, while *died* sounds more final.

EXERCISE **2** Wording

Insert the letter of the wording with the more positive connotation.

1. Andrew traveled to South America to interview a group of __b__.
   a. terrorists.   b. freedom fighters.

2. During the conference, the second grade teacher explained that Sarah
   would __b__.
   a. fail.   b. be offered another year in
                                                  second grade.

3. My uncle has managed to save millions of dollars because he is so __b__.
   a. cheap.   b. frugal.

Etymology

The dictionary entry for *home* that you studied begins with a history, or etymology, of the word. This information reveals the origin of the word in Middle English as well as its development before the twelfth century.

Sometimes the etymology involves word parts such as a prefix, root, or suffix. For other words, the etymology is tied to stories that provide a framework for the word. Often, knowing the story helps you remember the definition of the word. Study the following example from Greek mythology.

> **tantalize** \'tan-tə-līz\ vb –lized; -liz•ing [Tantalus} vt (1597) : to tease or torment by or as if by presenting something desirable to the view but continually keeping it out of reach ~vt : to cause one to be tantalized.

Source: By permission from *Merriam-Webster's Collegiate Dictionary*, 11th edition ©2005 by Merriam-Webster, Incorporated (www.Merriam-Webster.com).

TANTALIZE

The word *tantalize* comes from the Greek myth about King Tantalus, a mortal who was convinced he was more powerful than Zeus. When the gods heard about this man's snobbish behavior, they decided to punish him. They bound his hands and feet and stood him in cool, clear water. Overhead were juicy grapes. However, whenever King Tantalus was thirsty, the water would rush away from his reach. Likewise, when he was hungry, the wind would sweep the grapes from him, even when he stretched. For eternity, he was teased, or tormented. *Tantalize* means *to tease*.

As punishment for his excessive pride, the king was *tantalized* by the sight of the refreshing grapes and water, but he was never allowed to have them.

Source: Molly Gamble-Walker

Dictionary Skills Review

Read the following story, and underline each time you see the word *model* appear in the passage.

THE CASE OF THE MYSTERIOUS TREASURE

She was Nancy Drew and Veronica Mars rolled into one—unquestionably the most adept crime solver of the M-Generation (those multi-tasking Millennials). Able to complete homework, build a college résumé, attend classes, study for exams, and still unravel mysteries, Ima Best was invincible. Or so it seemed.

This new case, however, baffled her. And it was especially important for her to solve this because the reward was $50,000—enough to pay for most of her future college tuition, room, and board.

This case involved a map and a treasure. The only guide, however, was a mysterious letter, filled with clues, so unclear that no one had yet located the money. Ima had studied the letter for days, trying several angles. Now she was nearly ready to give up. Nearly.

However, just as any good idea comes subconsciously when you are doing those mundane chores like washing dishes or scrubbing floors, Ima happened on an idea while sipping her morning coffee and finishing the daily crossword puzzle.

"Words!" she said just loud enough for her cat M'aidez to stir briefly. "That just might be it," she added.

Recalling that the treasure was left by the philanthropist Treat Wiseman, a man who had made his living first as a journalist abroad and then as a creator of crossword puzzles, she knew that Mr. Wiseman probably used words as the basis of his clues.

Ima pulled out the letter and read again. She had thought the first line contained a typo, but now she realized it was the first of the clues. Everyone had read the line as "It is a sad world," but Treat Wiseman never made an error; he was the perfect writer.

"This has to be a clue!"

Friends,

It is a sad word we face, but I hope you will find comfort in the game I have planned with this <u>model</u> of my original letter. I have traveled the world and studied people the way a contractor studies an architect's <u>model</u> of a new building, or the way a meteorologist studies his computer <u>models</u> to predict the weather. Once, as a boy, I considered becoming a city planner and worked laboriously on a <u>model</u> of a town encompassed by railroad tracks, just like this wonderful town I started in. That is when I also thought of creating a <u>model</u> for the plans of a great skyscraper. Still, the <u>model</u> of one design seems to be the same as the <u>model</u> of another design. I wanted more, so I decided to travel. Never did I falter in my dream to travel the world—except for the year in Paris when I fell in love with a runway <u>model</u> . . . But I digress.

My message to you is to get an education, read daily, follow your heart, find your niche, and dream big. Then find a train and make it happen. I will not wish you luck. To succeed, you will need more than luck.

My best,

Treat Wiseman

Ima began to underline each time the word *model* appeared in the letter. "This has to be more than a coincidence," she mused. With her dictionary at hand, she studied the entry for the word.

"Yahoo!" she shouted, making M'aidez jump for cover. "I've solved it! I know the address! And I know where to look once I'm there!"

You Are the Detective

To determine the location of the $50,000, Ima first identified the number of the dictionary definition that corresponded to each use of the word *model*. Then she changed the number of the definition to a corresponding letter of the alphabet. For example, 1 = A, 2 = B, 3 = C.

Next, she checked her town map to find the street on which she should begin her search. Finally, because of the date in the word history provided in the dictionary excerpt and what Ima already knew about the crossword puzzle magnate, Treat Wiseman, she determined in which building to begin her search. Study the excerpt below to determine where Ima began her search to find the treasure.

> **mod•el** \mä-dəl\n [MF *modelle,* fr. Olt *modello,* fr. VL **modellus,* fr. L *modulus* small measure, fr. *modus*] (1575) **1** *obs* : a set of plans for a building **2** dial Brit : COPY, IMAGE **3** : structural design <a home on the ~ of an old farmhouse> **4** : a *usu.* Miniature representation of something *also* : a pattern of something to be made **5** : an example for imitation or emulation **6** : a person or thing that serves as a pattern for an artist; esp : one who poses for an artist **7** : ARCHETYPE **8** : an organism whose appearance a mimic imitates **9** : one who is employed to display clothes or other merchandise **10a** : a type or design of clothing b : a type or design (as a car) **11** : a description or analogy used to help visualize something (as an atom) that cannot be directly observed **12** : a system of postulates, data, and inferences presented as a mathematical description of an entity or state of affairs; also : a computer simulation based on such a system <climate ~s> **13** VERSION **14:** ANIMAL MODEL

Source: By permission from *Merriam-Webster's Collegiate Dictionary,* 11th edition ©2005 by Merriam-Webster, Incorporated (www.Merriam-Webster.com).

Step 1: Write the number of each definition that corresponds to the context in the letter.

<u> 2 </u>   <u> 1 </u>   <u> 12 </u>   <u> 4 </u>   <u> 1 </u>   <u> 3 </u>   <u> 3 </u>   <u> 9 </u>

Step 2: Write the letter of the alphabet that corresponds to the numbers in Step 1.

<u> B </u>   <u> A </u>   <u> L </u>   <u> D </u>   <u> A </u>   <u> C </u>   <u> C </u>   <u> I </u>

Step 3: Mark the spot on the map, and in the space below, explain how Ima knew which house number to check.

She knew the house number because of the year the word was listed in the etymology.

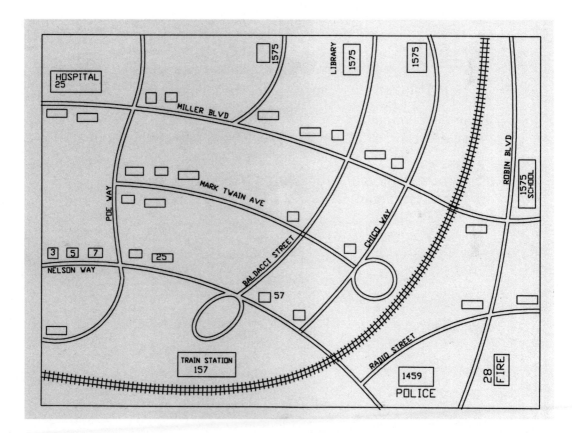

Stop and Think

Go to **www.dictionary.com** and **www.etymonline.com** to view online resources for the word *amplify*, then answer the following:

1. Which one provides the phonetic spelling of a word? dictionary.com

2. Which one provides the part of speech for the word? dictionary.com

3. Which one provides synonyms? dictionary.com

4. Which one provides antonyms?

Neither (unless you select the thesaurus feature)

5. Which one provides the history of the word? Both

(Answers 1–5: Both sites provide all of the information)

Go to the following Website and discover 300 ways to say "said." Then, in the space below, write ten ways you could use this information in future writing to avoid making your paper sound boring.

http://www.smcm.edu/writingcenter/Resources/rec_writers/ rev_cite/saysaid.htm

1

Review Test
Chapters 1 – 2

1 Word Parts

Match the definitions in Column 2 to the word parts in Column 1.

Column 1	Column 2
_f_ **1.** spect (inspect)	a. life
_h_ **2.** graph (autograph)	b. year
_k_ **3.** anti- (antidote)	c. two
_p_ **4.** magni (magnify)	d. state; condition
_r_ **5.** auto- (automobile)	e. feeling
_e_ **6.** path (sympathy)	f. look
_s_ **7.** ex- (export)	g. make; do; cause to become
_q_ **8.** –able (comfortable)	h. write; draw
_l_ **9.** –cide (homicide)	i. strong
_g_ **10.** –ize (digitize)	j. around
_a_ **11.** bio (biology)	k. against
_n_ **12.** photo (photography)	l. kill
_i_ **13.** forc (enforce)	m. between
_j_ **14.** circum- (circumference)	n. light
_o_ **15.** pater (paternal)	o. father
_c_ **16.** di- (divorce)	p. large
_m_ **17.** inter- (intersection)	q. able to
_t_ **18.** neo (neonatal)	r. self
_d_ **19.** –hood (childhood)	s. out; from
_b_ **20.** ann (annual)	t. new

43

1 **2 Context Clues**

Using context clues, select the letter of the best definition of the word in **bold** print.

___c___ **1.** Why is it that we are full of energy when cheering for our favorite football team late on a Friday night, but sitting in a Monday morning lecture **enervates** us?
a. interests   c. weakens
b. creates   d. strengthens

___a___ **2.** When David unexpectedly met the newspaper editor in the elevator, the encounter proved **auspicious** because he was able to schedule an interview for an internship.
a. favorable   c. dull
b. disappointing   d. new

___b___ **3.** Although Jean is confident and gracious in social settings, her brother Aaron feels **gauche** and uncomfortable.
a. graceful   c. sociable
b. awkward   d. outgoing

___c___ **4.** To **allay** our concerns about the hiking trip, our father promised to pack a fire extinguisher and first aid kit.
a. stir   c. ease
b. ignore   d. upset

___a___ **5.** Experts suggest a variety of ways to **pacify** a crying baby such as swaddling (wrapping the baby cocoon-style in a light blanket), rocking, singing, strolling, and cooing softly.
a. soothe   c. disturb
b. feed   d. trouble

___b___ **6.** Because the ballroom was filled with photographers, all of the city council members were **abstemious** about eating and drinking alcohol in public.
a. careless   c. fragile
b. moderate   d. lazy

___c___ **7.** Although he will accept employees having secrets, our supervisor will not **abide** his workers telling lies.
a. encircle   c. put up with
b. interview   d. surround

1

_____d_____ **8.** When we started our debate, I thought I had the stronger argument; however, I had to **concede** when my opponent gave a convincing conclusion.
- a. write
- b. wish
- c. sing
- d. give in

_____c_____ **9.** After sixteen-year-old Robin Graham **circumnavigated** the globe in his sailboat, he detailed his experiences in the book *Dove*.
- a. ignored
- b. avoided
- c. circled
- d. flattened

_____a_____ **10.** When he spotted a young man sleeping during his lecture on *Hamlet,* Dr. Fehrenbach walked up the auditorium steps and **lambasted** the student, saying, "I will not allow someone to show such disrespect in my class. Either wake up or leave!"
- a. criticized
- b. honored
- c. complimented
- d. tested

3 Context Clues and Roots

Step 1: Identify the type of context clue presented in the sentence and underline the word(s) you used to determine the definition of the word in **bold** print; then write the definition of the word part(s).

Step 2: Select the letter of the definition of the word.

1. I can **speculate** what your grade will be, but it will only be a guess.

Context Clue: synonym

Word Parts: *spec*: look, watch ; *-ate*: make

_____b_____ **Speculate** means
- a. find.
- b. guess.
- c. calculate.
- d. regret.

2. In some countries, voting rights are **circumscribed** by the ruling party, so there is never a chance to select someone new who can make a change in the government.

Context Clue: general context

Word Parts: *circum*: around ; *scrib*: write

_____a_____ **Circumscribe** means
- a. restrict.
- b. free.
- c. receive.
- d. promise.

1

3. Recently, Andy was faced with a **dilemma:** He had to make a difficult choice about whether to begin graduate school in the summer, taking classes two nights a week and finishing in six years, or quit his job and borrow money to finish in half the time.

   Context Clue: <u>synonym</u>   Word Part: *di-:* <u>two</u>

   <u>c</u>   **Dilemma** means
       a. education.
       b. recreation.
                      c. hard decision.
                      d. job.

4. Occasionally, everyone needs a little **solitude** instead of always being in crowds and the busy atmosphere of work and school.

   Context Clue: <u>antonym</u>   Word Part: *sol:* <u>alone</u>

   <u>d</u>   **Solitude** means
       a. noise.
       b. business.
                      c. gathering.
                      d. aloneness.

5. "Use your thesaurus," our writing teacher said, "so you can avoid repeating words that could be replaced with **synonyms** that mean the same thing."

   Context Clue: <u>general context</u>   Word Part: *nym:* <u>name</u>

   <u>a</u>   **Synonym** means
       a. word that has the same meaning.
       b. word that has the opposite meaning.
       c. word with a complex meaning.
       d. word with a double meaning.

6. If the government loses control, we will have no order; instead, we will have **anarchy**.

   Context Clue: <u>antonym</u>

   Word Parts *an:* <u>without</u>   ; *arch:* <u>leader</u>

   <u>c</u>   **Anarchy** means
       a. creative government.
       b. full authority.
                      c. disorder without leadership.
                      d. order with new leadership.

7. Following our dog's surgery, the veterinarian said, "Call me if you notice some **abnormal** behavior such as oversleeping, imbalances while walking, or a lack of appetite."

Context Clue: example   Word Part: *ab*: away; from

___a___ **Abnormal** means
   a. unusual.   c. typical.
   b. ordinary.   d. unnecessary.

8. Nursing students must take Anatomy and **Physiology** I, which is the study of biology that deals with the function of organs, tissues, and cells.

Context Clue: general context

Word Part: *-ology*: science or study of

___b___ **Physiology** means
   a. science of physics.
   b. science of the normal function of living things.
   c. study of stars.
   d. study of fossils.

9. Any gift of **remembrance** such as flowers, candy, or acts of kindness deserve a handwritten thank-you note.

Context Clue: example   Word Part: *-ance*: state of

___c___ **Remembrance** means
   a. science of thinking.   c. state of remembering.
   b. science of writing.   d. state of forgetting.

10. We realized the game would be a very physical one when the referees failed to **intervene** and step in to call some of the most obvious fouls.

Context Clue: general context   Word Part: *inter*: between

___d___ **Intervene** means
   a. move behind.   c. relax.
   b. rewind.   d. go between.

1

4 Dictionary Guide Words

Select the letter of the two entries in each set that would be the guide words appearing at the top of a dictionary page.

a / d   **1.** a. day-to-day   b. dead horse   c. day trader
              d. dead letter   e. deacon

b / e   **2.** a. factor   b. facing   c. fade
              d. factual   e. Fahrenheit

d / e   **3.** a. Ivy Leaguer   b. jab   c. jackal
              d. ivy   e. jacket

a / b   **4.** a. mast   b. mat   c. master
              d. masthead   e. mastodon

b / c   **5.** a. whatever   b. wetland   c. wheat
              d. whatsoever   e. whale

5 Phonetics

Write out the quotations that are spelled phonetically here.

1. "ə wĭn′ür nĕv′ür wīnz"—Paul Brown

"A winner never whines."—Paul Brown

2. "thə wĭl tōō wĭn ĭz ĭm′pör′tənt, bŭt thə wĭl tōō prĭ-pâr′ ĭz vīt′l."—Joe Paterno

"The will to win is important, but the will to prepare is vital."—Joe Paterno

3. "thə dĭf′ər-əns bĭ-twēn′ ə sək-sĕs′fəl pûr′sən ənd ŭth′ərz ĭz nŏt ə lăk ŭv strĕngkth, nŏt ə lăk ŭv nŏl′ĭj, bŭt ră*th*′ər ə lăk ŭv wĭl." —Vince Lombardi

"The difference between a successful person and others is not a lack of strength,

not a lack of knowledge, but rather a lack of will."—Vince Lombardi

4. "yōō dōnt hăv tōō burn bŏoks tōō dĭ-stroi ə kŭl′chər. jŭst gĕt pēpəl tōō stŏp rēd′ĭng *th*ĕm."—Ray Bradbury

"You don't have to burn books to destroy a culture. Just get people to stop

reading them."—Ray Bradbury

5. "thrō yŏŏr drēmz ĭn'too̅ spās līk ə kīt, ənd yoo̅ doo̅ nŏt nō hwŏt ĭt wĭl brĭng băk, ə noo̅ līf, ə noo̅ frĕnd, ə noo̅ lŭv, ə noo̅ kŭn'trē." –Anais Nin

"Throw your dreams into space like a kite, and you do not know what it will

bring back, a new life, a new friend, a new love, a new country."—Anais Nin

Source: http://www.quoteland.com

6 Dictionary Usage

*Use your dictionary to answer the following questions.

1. What is the first definition of the word *ambiguous*? doubtful, uncertain

2. What is the part of speech for the French term *carte blanche*? adj.

3. How many definitions are listed for *ear*? seven

4. How many syllables are in the word *stolid*? two

5. What does *stolid* mean? having or expressing little or no sensibility; unemotional

6. What is a synonym for *stolid*? impassive

7. Around what year did the word *stolid* first appear? 1600

8. Which word does *stolid* rhyme with? a. stolen b. solid b

9. What two parts of speech can the word *esteem* be? noun; verb

10. What is an example of the use of *esteem*? The esteem we all feel for her is great.

*Suggested answers are based on *Merriam-Webster's Collegiate Dictionary*, 11th ed.

3

Vocabulary and the Mind and Body Connection

Get Ready to Read About the Mind and Body Connection

In the previous chapters you learned that context clues and word analysis can help you determine the meanings of new words. In this chapter, you will draw on that information to determine the definitions of ten words used in an excerpt about health. The vocabulary in health textbooks can be very specialized and sometimes seems like it is from another languages. Therefore, a quick review of some word parts will be helpful.

First, identify the definitions of the following word parts by filling in the blanks:

1. The prefix *en-* means <u>within, in</u>.

2. The root *phys* means <u>body</u> as in *physical education* and *physician*.

3. The word *anxious* comes from the same root as *anxiety* and means *full of anxiety* or *concern*. However, many word experts now also approve of using the word *anxious* as a synonym for *eager*.

4. The suffix *–ate* means <u>cause to become</u> and indicates a <u>verb</u>.

5. The suffix *–ical* means <u>like or having the characteristics of</u> and indicates an
<u>adjective</u>.

Next, use the SAGE context clues as you consider the words in the
passage below.

alleviate	catharsis	enhance	nutrient	prompt
anxiety	endorphin	immune	physiological	torso

THE HEALING POWER OF LAUGHTER

It may surprise you to learn that a good joke can do far more than just
"tickle your funny bone." In fact, studies have shown that humor and laughter can improve your physical and mental health. Laughter is beneficial because it **prompts** stress reduction, pain relief, an **enhanced** immune system,
and a healthier outlook on life.

Laughter, like crying, is a form of **catharsis.** It provides an outlet for you
to **alleviate** feelings of stress and **anxiety.** Laughter can help "clear your
head," helping you to look at a situation from a new angle.

Studies show that laughter provides many **physiological** benefits. It
causes a temporary increase in your heart rate and blood pressure, which aids
in the delivery of oxygen and **nutrients** to your entire body. Laughter can also
help relax tense muscles in your face, shoulders, and **torso,** according to Allen
Klein, author of *The Healing Power of Humor.* And it exercises abdominal muscles.

Laughter helps the body produce new **immune** cells faster. Klein also
believes that a boosted immune system will help you fight off many illnesses,
including colds, flu, and even cancer.

Several studies have shown that exposing people to humorous experiences greatly improves their ability to deal with pain. When you laugh, Klein
suggests, your brain releases **endorphins**—the body's natural pain killers.

To fully gain the benefits of humor, you need to seek opportunities to
add humor to your life. Go see a funny movie. Watch your favorite sit-com;
grab the funny pages out of the Sunday paper or make funny faces in the mir-
ror with your kids.

—From "The Healing Power of Humor," *Living Healthy:*
Working Well, a monthly newsletter distributed to State of
California LAP Coordinators, May 1999. (Originally from
The Healing Power of Humor by Allen Klein, copyright©
1989 by Allen Klein, published by Jeremy P. Tarcher, a
member of Penguin Putnam Inc.)

VISUAL VOCABULARY

This family is enjoying the

___b___ benefits of laughter as well as creating a memorable bonding.

   a. physiological
   b. immune

Courtesy of Microsoft.

EXERCISE 1 Context Clues

A. Refer to the previous passage and use context clues from the sentences below to determine the definition of each of the following words in **bold** print. Do not consult a dictionary.

1. alleviate (ə-lē′vē-āt′) v.
Anna was able to **alleviate** her headache with a new pain reliever that contained aspirin.

___c___ **Alleviate** means
   a. avoid.
   b. increase.
               c. relieve.
               d. continue.

2. anxiety (ăng-zī′ĭ-tē) n.
Students who have test **anxiety** tend to worry about the outcome instead of focusing on the learning process.

___a___ **Anxiety** means
   a. fear.
   b. pleasure.
               c. relationship.
               d. joy.

3. catharsis (kə-thär′sĭs)n.
Standing on the steps outside the biology lab, Evan gave a loud whoop—the sudden letting go of tension that had built up over the semester was a welcome **catharsis.**

___d___ **Catharsis** means
- a. harshness.
- b. silence.
- c. creativity.
- d. release.

4. endorphin (ĕn-dôr′fĭn) n.
After 20 minutes of intense workout, Allen began to develop a more positive outlook, a result of the brain's release of **endorphins**.

___a___ **Endorphin** means
- a. group of hormones that produce a sense of well-being.
- b. group of hormones that affect growth.
- c. cancer cells.
- d. microscopic organisms.

5. enhance (ĕn-hăns′) v.
Before putting their home on the market, the young couple followed their realtor's advice to **enhance** the curb appeal of their home and increase its value.

___b___ **Enhance** means
- a. invent.
- b. improve.
- c. end.
- d. begin.

6. immune (to) (ĭ-myo͞on′) adj.
Adam felt he was **immune** to most germs in his office because he cleaned his desk and phone daily with bleach wipes and used a hand sanitizer after shaking hands with any co-workers.

___a___ **Immune** means
- a. resistant.
- b. constant.
- c. available.
- d. struggling.

7. nutrient (no͞o′trē-ənt,) n.
Nutritionists recommend steaming vegetables to prevent a loss of **nutrients** through overcooking.

___b___ **Nutrients** are
- a. harmful effects.
- b. nourishing ingredients.
- c. careless results.
- d. colorful ingredients.

8. physiological (fĭz′ē-ə-lŏj′ĭ-kəl) adj.
   Physiological problems such as tension headaches and neck pain can develop when we allow mental stress to be a constant factor in our lives.

   ___c___ **Physiological** means
   a. characteristic of mental disorders.
   b. characteristic of the mind.
   c. physical characteristics of living things.
   d. physical characteristics of nonliving things.

9. prompt (prŏmpt) v.
   Receiving an A on his essay after laboring for hours in the library **prompted** Elias to continue his successful study routine.

   ___c___ **Prompt** means
   a. lower.   c. cause.
   b. agree.   d. get rid of.

10. torso (tôr′sō) n.
    The principal sponsored a fashion show to present the new dress code, which included shirts that fall below the waist to avoid exposed **torsos.**

    ___a___ **Torso** means
    a. stomach area.   c. elbows.
    b. ankles.   d. knees.

EXERCISE 2 Word Sorts

Synonyms

Match the word to the synonyms or definitions that follow each blank.

1. __physiological__ biological; vital; having to do with living things; organic

2. __nutrient__ nourishment; food; ingredient of sustenance; enrichment

3. __endorphins__ hormones that produce a sense of well-being and reduce pain sensation

4. __catharsis__ release; suspension; cleansing; unburdening

5. __torso__ trunk; stomach area

Antonyms

Select the letter of the word(s) with the opposite meaning.

_c_ **6.** prompt
- a. encourage
- b. steer
- c. stop
- d. change

_a_ **7.** anxiety
- a. confidence
- b. worry
- c. illness
- d. slavery

_c_ **8.** alleviate
- a. ease
- b. raise
- c. worsen
- d. leave

_d_ **9.** immune
- a. foreign
- b. protected
- c. steady
- d. at risk

_d_ **10.** enhance
- a. improve
- b. encourage
- c. cause interest
- d. make worse

EXERCISE **3** Fill in the Blank

Use context clues to determine the word that best completes each sentence.

1. We were fascinated by the man who had tattooed the Battle of Waterloo on his torso _____, displaying a navel ring in the center.

2. Scientists now believe that some animals share the same kinds of physiological _____ disorders as humans when they suffer from stress.

3. If you exercise long enough, your brain will release endorphins _____, which will create a sense of well-being.

4. Most people have a sense of humor and enjoy the catharsis _____ that laughter provides in releasing tension.

5. If you want to lose weight, choose foods high in nutrients _____ such as fruits and vegetables, exercise 30 minutes a day three times a week, and avoid snacking two to three hours before bedtime.

6. To alleviate _____ pain and ease the swelling in a pulled muscle, follow the RICE steps of rest, ice, compression, and elevation.

7. People who have a negative outlook on life and focus on their fears and concerns can learn to handle their <u>anxiety</u> by engaging in positive self-talk and choosing upbeat friends.

8. Exercise and a good diet can <u>enhance</u> your appearance as well as improve your health.

9. Vitamin C, which is found in strawberries, oranges, and grapefruit, can boost your <u>immune</u> system and help you resist infections.

10. Although heart patients report that surgery <u>prompts</u> them to avoid foods high in fat right after their hospital stay, they often begin to slide back into bad habits later.

EXERCISE 4 Application

Using context clues, insert the vocabulary word in the appropriate blank. A part-of-speech clue is given for each vocabulary word.

The Surgeon General has begun a major campaign to fight obesity in America. By teaching about the **(1)** (adj.) <u>physiological</u> benefits of exercise and choosing proper **(2)** (n.) <u>nutrient(s)</u> in meal planning, parents as well as school and health officials aim to **(3)** (v.) <u>alleviate</u> the problem. What has **(4)** (v.) <u>prompt(ed)</u> the concern is the growing number of younger Americans who are developing Type 2 diabetes as well as behavior and learning problems as a result of their diet and lack of physical activity. The medical community explains that people who watch TV or play video games regularly rather than choose to exercise fail to get the benefits of an **(5)** (adj.) <u>immune</u> system that is **(6)** (v.) <u>enhance(d)</u> and improved through simple weight-bearing activities such as walking. Often, these same people accumulate fat deposits in their **(7)** (n.) <u>torso</u>, which can lead to early heart attacks. Also, because they have no vigorous exercise, they miss the feeling of calm and well-being that occurs when the body's **(8)** (n.) <u>endorphin(s)</u> kick

in after 20 or 30 minutes of vigorous exercise. Instead of feeling a
(9) (n.) <u>catharsis</u>, or release, because they have had a good workout, they develop **(10)** (adj.) <u>anxiety</u> and fear as a result of
watching programs with violent content.

Stop and Think

A. Using at least three words from the list, summarize the passage in 30 words or less in the space below.

<u>Humor promotes good health by **alleviating anxiety**, releasing tension, increasing</u>

<u>the delivery of oxygen and **nutrients** to the body, and exercising your **torso**</u>

<u>muscles.   (24 words)</u>

B. Use a highlighter to color in the circles next to the words you can define without looking at the definitions, and then pair up with a classmate to share your answers.

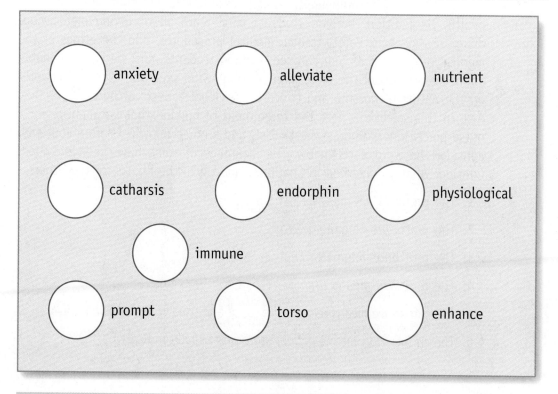

4 Vocabulary and Nursing

Get Ready to Read About Vocabulary and Nursing

College nursing textbooks cover a range of topics such as the history of nursing, pain management, community health concerns, ways to promote good health, life-span development, communicating with patients, and assessing health. In addition, nursing students must learn about giving medication, diagnostic systems, safety issues, medical procedures, and the ethics of the medical profession. As you can see, nursing students must be knowledgeable about many areas of the profession. The following selection is from a chapter on the nature of nursing and concerns the legal aspects of nursing practice. Also in this selection, note the three areas of nursing that are mentioned: a nurse-practitioner, a nurse-anesthetist, and a nurse-midwife. Before you read, consider the word parts below. The meanings of some have been provided. Consider what you learned in Chapter 1 and fill in the blanks for the others.

1. The prefix *inter-* means between.
2. The prefix *pro-* means forward.
3. The root *gnos* means *to know.*
4. The root *vita* means *life.*
5. The suffix *–ive* means *related, like,* or *of* and usually indicates an adjective.
6. The suffix *–tion* means *action, state* and usually indicates a noun.

| alternative | imperative | intervention | obtain | prognosis |
| consent | imply | invasive | procedure | vital |

INFORMED CONSENT

Informed **consent** is an agreement by a client to accept a course of treatment or a **procedure** after being provided complete information, including the benefits and risks of treatment, **alternatives** to the treatment, and **prognosis** if not treated by a health care provider. Usually the client signs a form provided by the agency. The form is a record for the informed consent, not the informed consent itself.

There are two types of consent: express and **implied**. Express consent may be either an oral or written agreement. Usually, the more **invasive** a procedure and/or the greater the potential for risk to the client, the greater the need for written permission. Implied consent exists when the individual's nonverbal behavior indicates agreement. For example, clients who position their bodies for an injection or cooperate with the taking of **vital** signs suggest implied consent. Consent is also implied in a medical emergency when an individual cannot provide express consent because of a physical condition.

Obtaining informed consent for specific medical and surgical treatments is the responsibility of the person who is going to perform the procedure. Generally it is the physician; however, it could be a nurse practitioner, nurse-anesthetist, or nurse-midwife who is performing the procedures in their advanced practices.

Informed consent also applies to nurses who are not independent practitioners and are performing direct nursing care for such procedures as nasogastric tube insertion or medication administration. The nurse relies on orally expressed consent or implied consent for most nursing **interventions.** It is **imperative** to remember the importance of communicating with the client by explaining nursing procedures, ensuring the client understands, and obtaining permission.

—*Source:* Kozier, Barbara, Glenora Erb, Audrey Berman, &
Shirley Snyder, *The Fundamentals of Nursing*, 7th ed.,
Prentice-Hall, 2004, pp. 52-53.

VISUAL VOCABULARY

Learning to use a computer is

_____b_____ for college students to succeed in classes, especially if they have to do research or write papers frequently.

  a. invasive
  b. imperative

Susan Pongratz

EXERCISE **1** Context Clues

Refer to the previous passage and use context clues from the sentences below to determine the definition of each of the following words in **bold** print. Do not consult a dictionary.

1. alternative (ôl-tûr′nə-tĭv) n.
   In addition to medication, some people seek **alternatives** for pain management such as acupuncture and meditation.

   _____b_____ **Alternative** means
       a. target.   c. reason.
       b. choice.   d. satisfaction.

2. consent (kən-sĕnt′) n.
   Before he proposed to his girlfriend, Barrett went to see her father to ask for his **consent,** knowing that with his blessing and permission, their marriage would be off to a good start.

   _____c_____ **Consent** means
       a. selection.   c. permission.
       b. wonder.   d. mission.

3. imperative (ĭm-pĕr′ə-tĭv) adj.

It is **imperative** that people read in order to develop ideas of their own based on facts rather than form their opinions from what other people tell them to believe.

___a___ **Imperative** means

    a. important.   c. disappointing.

    b. simple.   d. surprise.

4. imply (ĭm-plī′) v.

"When you told me you have never believed anything I have said," asked Adam, "did you intend to **imply** that I have never been trustworthy?"

___d___ **Imply** means

    a. discourage.   c. conclude.

    b. imagine.   d. hint.

5. intervention (ĭn′tər-vĕn′shən) n.

Although Shana was having some difficulty in her classes, her counselor arranged for a learning coach to offer some **intervention** and provide other ways to help her improve her academic performance.

___b___ **Intervention** means

    a. peace.   c. formality.

    b. stepping in.   d. independence.

6. invasive (ĭn-vā′sĭv) adj.

Because Marian's surgery was **invasive**, she was not able to go home the same day, and her recovery time was much longer than she had expected because the surgeon used ten staples to close the incision.

___a___ **Invasive** means

    a. entered by puncture or incision.   c. uncomplicated.

    b. easy.   d. unsafe.

7. obtain (əb-tān′) v.

To **obtain** a driver's license, you will need to provide a birth certificate and proof of residency.

___c___ **Obtain** means

    a. give.   c. get.

    b. donate.   d. salute.

8. procedure (pər-sē'jər) n.
Because of the results of his stress test, Rusty was scheduled for a follow-up **procedure** to determine if he had a blockage in one of his arteries.

_____a_____ **Procedure** means
 a. operation.   c. production.
 b. creation.   d. invention.

9. prognosis (prŏg-nō'sĭs) n.
Following the surgery, we waited to talk with the doctor to determine the **prognosis** for what we could expect concerning our father's recovery.

_____d_____ **Prognosis** means
 a. arrangement.   c. qualification.
 b. necessity.   d. prediction.

10. vital (vīt'l) adj.
The heart is a **vital** organ, so we should take measures to protect it with diet and exercise.

_____b_____ **Vital** means
 a. unnecessary.   c. old.
 b. necessary for life. d. awakened.

EXERCISE 2 Word Sorts

Synonyms

Match the word to the synonyms or definitions that follow each blank.

1. procedure _____ plan; method; process; technique

2. prognosis _____ forecast; guess; expectation; prediction

3. alternative _____ substitute; option; choice; back-up

4. invasive _____ entered by an incision

5. imply _____ suggest; hint; mention; allude

Antonyms

Select the letter of the word(s) with the opposite meaning.

_____b_____ **6.** consent
 a. agreement   c. contract
 b. refusal   d. allowance

__b__   **7.** vital
   a. important
   b. unnecessary
   c. practical
   d. methodical

__a__   **8.** intervention
   a. avoidance
   b. involvement
   c. question
   d. exception

__c__   **9.** obtain
   a. get
   b. attain
   c. lose
   d. surprise

__c__   **10.** imperative
   a. urgent
   b. important
   c. unimportant
   d. necessary

EXERCISE 3 Fill in the Blank

Use context clues to determine the word that best completes each sentence.

1. The paramedic immediately checked the accident victim's <u>vital</u> signs, including heart rate, respiration, and blood pressure.

2. After more than 25 hours of surgery to separate the Banda twins who were conjoined at the head, Dr. Benjamin Carson was interviewed by journalists who had gathered in Medunsa, Zambia, eager to learn the surgeon's <u>prognosis</u> of the babies' future.

3. Following the surprising loss, the basketball coach simply said, "Never before have we been forced to play such a physical game"—by which he meant to <u>imply</u>, but did not state, "The referees were no good."

4. Before they could get married, Kim and Carlos had to <u>obtain</u> a marriage license.

5. It is popular for celebrities to get regular cosmetic <u>procedure(s)</u> with the goal of keeping their youthful good looks.

6. Before being allowed to participate in high school sports, parents are required to give their <u>consent</u> and agree not to sue the school if their child is injured.

7. "To lower your blood pressure," the doctor warned, "your only <u>alternative</u> to taking medicine is to change your lifestyle and diet."

8. If a person feels the signs of a heart attack, it is recommended that he or she take an aspirin as a quick <u>intervention</u> and then call 911.

9. "To avoid paying a penalty, it is <u>imperative</u> that we meet the deadline," announced our supervisor, "so we will have to continue working through the night until the project is complete."

10. With nuclear medicine, a patient's arteries can be explored with a radioactive chip, thus avoiding any <u>invasive</u> surgery.

EXERCISE 4 Application

Using context clues, insert the vocabulary word in the appropriate blank. A part-of-speech clue is given for each vocabulary word.

Do meditation and prayer contribute to healing? Some people think so. However, a recent study published in the *American Heart Journal* proves otherwise. In a study of more than 1,800 heart by-pass surgery patients who had other people praying for them, results of the subjects were no better than of those who had no one praying.

While there are those who doubt the probability that good thoughts can have good effects, other scientists have discovered their findings may **(1)** (v.) <u>imply</u> the opposite is true. First, people who are members of a religious order tend to consider it **(2)** (adj.) <u>imperative</u> that they take better care of their bodies. Also, it seems that people who are concerned about the lives of others tend not to focus on their own worries as much and thus seem happier; as a result, they often have a better **(3)** (n.) <u>prognosis</u>, or forecast, after a surgical **(4)** (n.) <u>procedure</u> than people who feel sorry for themselves. Likewise, whether a person practices Judaism, Christianity, Islam, Hinduism, Buddhism, or any other religion that includes prayer and meditation, it is recognized that these are a form of cleansing the mind that can sometimes provide an **(5)** (n.) alternative to extensive medication. This is not unlike the features of the Lamaze method of childbirth that uses relaxation and breathing techniques to overcome sensations of pain.

While some current evidence does not support the beliefs of some religions that recognize the mind/body/spirit connection, one study researched people who were facing **(6)** (adj.) invasive surgery or a major medical procedure that affected **(7)** (adj.) vital organs. These patients were prayed for and actually **(8)** (v.) obtain (ed) healing. The fascinating part is that they did not know they were being prayed for. This double-blind experiment was performed so that it would not affect the mental attitude of the patients, even if they had given their **(9)** (n.) consent for prayer. Scientists are in search of truth. It may be, though, that researchers may only prove that the **(10)** (n.) intervention of prayer is a communication of faith, not science.

Although some try to use prayer as an attempt to manipulate a higher being, scientists may end up proving what believers have known all along. Good thoughts relieve stress and can, therefore, produce good results. Believing, after all, is about faith. In the meantime, as one of the leaders of the most recent study, Jeffery Dusek of Harvard Medical School said, "No one single study is ever going to provide an answer."

—*Source:* Adapted from Stein, Rob, "New Study Puts No
Faith in Power of Healing Prayer," *The Washington Post*,
March 31, 2006.

Stop and Think

Visit **www.etymonline.com** and determine what words would best complete the following word histories.

1. imply

Around <u>1347</u>, the word *imply* meant <u>to enfold, enwrap, entangle</u>. It originally came from the <u>Latin</u> word *implicare*, which means *involve*. The definition *to involve something unstated as a logical conse-quence* was first recorded in <u>1529</u>.

2. obtain

Around <u>1425</u>, the word *obtenir* evolved from the <u>Latin</u> *obtinere*, which means *hold, take hold of, acquire*. The prefix *ob-* means <u>to</u> and the root *tenere* means <u>to hold</u>.

3. imperative

In <u>1530</u>, the word *imperative* appeared from the Latin <u>imperatus</u>, meaning *pertaining to a command* and *imperatus*, or <u>command</u>. The pre-fix *in-* means <u>in</u> and the root *parare* means <u>beget or bear</u>.

4. prognosis

In <u>1655</u>, the word *prognosis* meant *forecast of the probable course of a disease*. It came from the <u>Greek</u> word *prognosis*, which means <u>foreknowledge</u>. The prefix *pro-* means <u>before</u> and the root *gignoskein* means <u>come to know</u>.

5. alternative

The word *alternative*, which means <u>offering a choice</u>, first appeared in <u>1590</u>.

Study the pictures below and decide which vocabulary word from this chapter best summarizes the image. Write the word, the definition, and your reason for choosing the word. (Answers may vary.)

Word	Definition	Reason
1. consent		
2. vital		
3. intervention		
4. procedure		
5. invasive		

Vocabulary and Environmental Health

Get Ready to Read About Environmental Health

Your body is more than 50 percent water, so getting your eight glasses of water a day is important. Before you read about the trend to use bottled water, review some terms you will encounter in the reading, and then fill in the blanks with the definitions of word parts you studied in Chapter 1.

1. chlorination: the addition of small amounts of chlorine used to disinfect water.

2. fluoridation: the addition of the fluoride compound to prevent tooth decay.

3. The prefix *con-* means <u>with or together</u>.

4. The root *path* means <u>feeling</u>.

5. The root *stat* means *stand*.

6. The suffix *-ize* means <u>cause to become</u> and indicates a verb.

7. The suffix *-tion* means *condition* and indicates a noun.

| consumption | industrialize | pristine | quest | scarce |
| contaminate | pathogens | quench | recess | status |

BOTTLED WATER: CLEAN WATER IN
SCARCE SUPPLY

Consider the following: Water covers 71 percent of the globe's surface, but 98 percent of that water is too salty for human **consumption** without using extremely costly methods to make it more pure. That leaves just 2 percent available for us to drink, and that 2 percent is unevenly distributed around the world, with 60 percent of it located in just 10 countries. In addition, **industrialized** countries use far greater amounts than do other nations. As a result, fresh water is becoming a **scarce** product. Today about 1.2 billion people lack ways to get clean water and another 5 to 10 million (mostly women and children) die from illnesses related to water **contaminated** with solid wastes, chemicals, and other water-borne **pathogens**.

People in the United States are among the worse consumers of water, using an average of 150 gallons a day, compared with 50 gallons by Europeans and 7.5 gallons by Africans. Whether it is used to water lawns, to wash cars, or for the simple luxury of a daily bath, Americans often take water for granted. Yet we do seem to be aware that *clean* water is rare. A growing number of communities across the country have begun to raise objections over the chlorination and fluoridation of public drinking water. In our **quest** to find the best, most pure drinking water, we are moving increasingly to bottled water that promises to be from **pristine** wells springing from deep **recesses** in the Earth's crust. With its designer labels and names that promise to **quench** your thirst, bottled water has become associated with **status,** wealth, and a health-conscious society.

—Adapted from Donatelle, *Health: The Basics*, 4th ed., p. 384.

VISUAL VOCABULARY

These health professionals are wearing surgical masks to protect themselves and their patients by preventing airborne

___b___ from spreading.

a. quests
b. pathogens

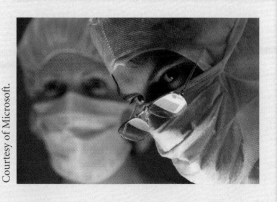

Courtesy of Microsoft.

EXERCISE **1** Context Clues

Refer to the previous passage and use context clues from the sentences below to determine the definition of each of the following words in **bold** print. Do not consult a dictionary.

1. consumption (kən-sŭmp′shən) n.
Consumption of four to five servings of fruits and vegetables a day is now recommended for a healthy diet.

___b___ **Consumption** means
    a. ignoring the signs.   c. a research study.
    b. eating and drinking.   d. traveling alone.

2. contaminate (kən-tăm′ə-nāt′) v.
To avoid eating any food that has been **contaminated**, follow guidelines for safe food preparation described at the Website of the Centers for Disease Control and Prevention at www.cdc.gov or go to www. fightbac.org.

___d___ **Contaminate** means
    a. tease.   c. understand.
    b. make clean.   d. infect.

3. industrialize (ĭn-dŭs′trē-ə-līz′) v.
Because of a lack of resources, third-world countries with no industries often rely on nations that are more **industrialized** for help in providing health care, sanitation, schools, roads, and bridges.

___a___ **Industrialize** means
    a. develop or organize with production or industry.
    b. feel compassion for those less fortunate.
    c. accept responsibility.
    d. focus on art and literature.

4. pathogen (păth′ə-jən) n.
EMTs are required to wear latex gloves and sometimes surgical masks to prevent infection by **pathogens** when transporting bleeding patients.

___a___ **Pathogen** means
    a. bacteria or fungus that causes disease.
    b. health worker.
    c. sanitary conditions.
    d. surgical procedure.

5. pristine (prĭs′tēn′) adj.

My grandmother can remember when the muddy, dark water of the James River was so clean and **pristine** that she could see the sandy bottom from the end of Hilton Pier.

   _c_   **Pristine** means

      a. unclean.   c. unspoiled.

      b. dangerous.   d. unusual.

6. quench (kwĕnch) v.

Next time, to **quench** your thirst, choose water instead of a soda because drinks with caffeine and sugar actually make you more thirsty.

   _c_   **Quench** means

      a. roll in a tight ball.   c. satisfy.

      b. survive in difficult times.   d. make active.

7. quest (kwĕst) n.

In the film _Life Aquatic_, the character Steve Zissou, who was played by Bill Murray, is on a **quest** to find the Jaguar Shark, which was responsible for his friend's death.

   _a_   **Quest** means

      a. search.   c. view.

      b. study.   d. management.

8. recess (rē′sĕs′) n.

In a **recess** in the church wall, Stuart found the famous statue sculpted by his favorite artist.

   _b_   **Recess** means

      a. doorway.   c. prize.

      b. a nook or indentation.   d. stolen goods.

9. scarce (skârs) adj.

After the hurricane, ice was so **scarce** that we had to stand in line for several hours just to get two bags.

   _c_   **Scarce** means

      a. plenty.   c. hard to find.

      b. noticeable.   d. exhausted.

10. status (stăt′əs) n.

Carrie's grandfather is a proud, hardworking man who believes you make your own **status** in life, rather than relying on someone else to define your social level.

___b___ **Status** means

    a. family.

    b. level or standing.

    c. improvement.

    d. question.

EXERCISE 2 Word Sorts

Synonyms

Match the word to the synonyms or definitions that follow each blank.

1. ___status_____ standing; position; rank; importance

2. ___pathogen_____ bacteria; fungus; contaminant

3. ___quest_____ search; hunt; mission; pursuit

4. ___consumption_____ eating; drinking; intake; ingestion

5. ___industrialize_____ develop; create industry; organize

Antonyms

Select the letter of the word(s) with the opposite meaning.

___d___ **6.** recess

    a. front

    b. indentation

    c. arch

    d. bulge

___b___ **7.** pristine

    a. clean

    b. dirty

    c. level

    d. organized

___d___ **8.** contaminate

    a. poison

    b. sweep

    c. settle

    d. make pure

___b___ **9.** quench

    a. satisfy

    b. make thirsty

    c. surround

    d. make calm

___a___ **10.** scarce

    a. plentiful

    b. limited

    c. afraid

    d. steady

EXERCISE **3** Fill in the Blank

Use context clues to determine the word that best completes each sentence.

1. Ella's parents never allowed a TV in the house because they did not want some of the shows to <u>contaminate</u> her mind with the violence and profanity that they viewed as polluting rather than educational.

2. After engaging in the <u>consumption</u> of 35 hot dogs in seven minutes at the county fair, Seth decided to wait 30 minutes before riding the Ferris wheel.

3. Although he was a newcomer, Ron was surprised that the other club members made him feel as if he shared their <u>status</u> instead of acting as if they had higher rank.

4. Nothing <u>quenches</u> my thirst in the summertime like an ice-cold cherry limeade.

5. If you were a new ruler of a poor country, what is the first area you would <u>industrialize</u> in order to help it develop and progress into a more prosperous nation?

6. When Tom pulled down the wallpaper in the dining room, he found a <u>recess</u> in one side, which was the perfect place for him to install a stereo speaker.

7. My favorite scene in one of the Indiana Jones films is when he is on a <u>quest</u> to find the Holy Grail and is forced to make the Leap of Faith.

8. Because food was so <u>scarce</u> in World War II, many people were given food coupons to control the sale of limited supplies.

9. Costa Rica is an environmentally concerned country that emphasizes recycling and the maintenance of <u>pristine</u> beaches, free of litter and pollution.

10. In 1918 and 1919, the Spanish flu caused between 20 and 40 million deaths as a result of <u>pathogens</u> rapidly spreading through physical contact with infected people.

EXERCISE **4** Application

Using context clues, insert the vocabulary word in the appropriate blank. A part-of-speech clue is given for each vocabulary word.

Arline sat in a **(1)** (n.) recess_____ in an area cut into the rock behind the waterfall, proud that she had found a **(2)** (adj.) pristine_____ pool, free of pollutants, which was clean enough to **(3)** (v.) quench_____ her thirst. Such pure water that was free of disease-causing **(4)** (n.) pathogens_____ was becoming very **(5)** (adj.) scarce_____, and with such an important natural resource in short supply, she realized the importance of her biology professor's caution about caring for the environment. After doing some research for the class, she decided to search for ways to protect the environment.

The problem, she soon discovered, was more complicated than she first believed. For example, to **(6)** (v.) industrialize_____ the previously financially depressed area and provide jobs for the local residents, factories had moved in and provided a source of economic development. However, the chemicals from the factories that saved the area from poverty had also **(7)** (v.) contaminated_____ the water downstream. Thus, water clean enough for **(8)** (n.) consumption_____ was becoming limited. One problem had replaced the other. Arline decided, though, that if she could educate the community and the factory owners, they could all work hand in hand and model environmentally safe procedures for other factories to follow. Her own **(9)** (n.) quest_____ for clean water could lead to a search for clean emissions from factories. As a result of her search, the little area in the mountains could be given important **(10)** (n.) status_____, raising its image in the eyes of other counties in the state. And all of this had begun with a research project in her college biology class.

Stop and Think

 Reread the passage "Bottled Water: Clean Water in Scarce Supply" and then, using two vocabulary words, summarize the selection in 30 words or less. (Answers will vary.)

Fresh water is becoming **scarce**. Because of chemicals, expensive purification, and

wasteful use, some are turning to bottled water, a **status** symbol of the rich. (25 words)

 Write a synonym for each word below and then draw a picture that represents the word. (Answers will vary.)

consumption	contaminate	pathogen
pristine	quest	status

6. Vocabulary and Longevity

Get Ready to Read About Longevity

The search for the fountain of youth has lured explorers and fortune hunters for centuries. What is the secret of living longer? Before you read about one theory, consider the word parts below. The meanings of some have been provided. Consider what you learned in Chapter 1 and fill in the blanks for the others.

1. The prefix *ana-* means *opposite*.

2. The prefix *contra-* means <u>against</u>.

3. The prefix *pre-* means <u>before</u>.

4. The root *gen* means *kind, gender, race, or stock*.

5. The root *homo* means *same*.

6. The suffix *–ic* means *like* or *similar to* and indicates an adjective.

7. The suffix *–ous* means <u>full of</u> and indicates an <u>adjective</u>.

access	contraception	culture	inherit	previous
analyze	counteract	homogeneous	longevity	socio-economic

SECRETS OF LONGEVITY

Waiting to have children may add years to a woman's life, says Jenni Pettay of the University of Turku in Finland. The evolutionary biologist **analyzed** 5,000 birth records from four generations of 17th- and 18th-century Finns and found that women who waited the longest before having their first child were statistically more likely to live longer. The delay in childbirth seems to be **inherited**: Late mothers' daughters also tended to become late mothers themselves. (Late was defined as after 30.)

Previous research has suggested that women who delay having children live longer. But none of these studies was able to determine if the **longevity** was due to cultural factors, such as a higher **socio-economic** class or better living conditions. Pettay got around those issues by studying women from a **homogeneous** population who did not have **access** to **contraception** or advanced medical care.

Still, Pettay says, it's **culture,** not genes that explains why Westerners delay parenthood: "In modern society there tends to be a low number of off-spring per couple, so natural selection isn't at work. But the study does suggest there may be benefits to later motherhood that evolved to **counteract** the decrease in total fertility, such as living longer to provide care to grandchildren."

—"Secrets of Longevity" by Jocelyn Selim, *Discover*, June 2005, Vol. 26, No. 6, p.14. Reprinted by permission of PARS International Corporation.

VISUAL VOCABULARY

Students who participate in sports begin a good habit of a healthy lifestyle and may increase their ___b___ to ensure a longer, healthier life.

a. culture
b. longevity

Courtesy of Microsoft.

EXERCISE **1** Context Clues

Refer to the previous passage and use context clues from the sentences below to determine the definition of each of the following words in **bold** print. Do not consult a dictionary.

1. access (ăk′sĕs) n.
In order to get **access** to the college library's online collections, you will need a log-in name and password that is available only to students.

    __b__   **Access** means
      a. end.   c. outlet.
      b. admission.   d. hallway.

2. analyze (ăn′ə-līz′) v.
William tried to **analyze** a situation carefully before making a decision.

    __d__   **Analyze** means
      a. encourage.   c. warn.
      b. harm.   d. examine.

3. contraception (kŏn′trə-sĕp′shən) n.
The availability of methods of **contraception** now make it possible for couples to plan a pregnancy.

    __c__   **Contraception** means
      a. responsibility.   c. method of birth control.
      b. parenthood.   d. freedom of choice.

4. counteract (koun′tər-ăkt′) v.
Helen relies on her medication to **counteract** the effects of her spring allergies.

    __a__   **Counteract** means
      a. overcome.   c. increase gradually.
      b. discuss.   d. consider carefully.

5. culture (kŭl′chər) n.
A good **culture** on a college campus has an atmosphere of learning that focuses on the students rather than the politics of the administration.

    __c__   **Culture** means
      a. campus.   c. environment.
      b. learning.   d. library.

6. homogeneous (hŏ′mə-jē′nē-əs) adj.

By arranging people in a **homogenous** group, the scientist was sure the sample of people he studied consisted of similar types.

___b___ **Homogeneous** means
   a. opinionated.
   b. having some like characteristics.
   c. identical.
   d. different.

7. inherit (ĭn-hĕr′ĭt) v.

Sadly, some people eagerly anticipate the items they will **inherit** even before their relatives have died and the last will and testament is read.

___b___ **Inherit** means
   a. to lend for a short time.   c. to settle a difference.
   b. to receive as a gift.   d. to buy for a good price.

8. longevity (lŏn-jĕv′ĭ-tē) n.

To increase the **longevity** of your car, be sure to change the oil every 3,000 miles and maintain proper tire pressure.

___d___ **Longevity** means
   a. degree of happiness.   c. attractiveness.
   b. an impossibility.   d. lifespan.

9. previous (prē′vē-əs) adj.

In **previous** semesters, Stephanie had struggled in college classes; however, this semester, she adopted new study strategies that helped her become an active, successful learner.

___a___ **Previous** means
   a. earlier.   c. next.
   b. following.   d. unsuccessful.

10. socio-economic (sō′sē-ō-ĕk′ə-nŏm′ĭk) adj.

Test scores in public schools often reflect the **socio-economic** backgrounds of their students, and real estate agents often use this information to market homes in a particular neighborhood.

___a___ **Socio-economic** means
   a. related to financial and social level of a group.
   b. related to government waste.
   c. having to do with fun.
   d. associated with hard work.

EXERCISE **2** Word Sorts

Synonyms

Match the word to the synonyms or definitions that follow each blank.

1. longevity _____ long life; endurance, prolonged existence; lifespan

2. access _____ reach; admission; entrance; passage

3. culture _____ society; environment; atmosphere; lifestyle

4. contraception _____ birth control; pregnancy prevention; family planning

5. socio-economic _____ social and financial status; rank; level; hierarchy

Antonyms

Select the letter of the word(s) with the opposite meaning.

___a___ **6.** previous
      a. afterward   c. before
      b. first   d. interrupted

___b___ **7.** analyze
      a. consider   c. suspend
      b. ignore   d. develop

___a___ **8.** inherit
      a. give   c. enjoy
      b. receive   d. take over

___c___ **9.** counteract
      a. cancel   c. cause
      b. prevent   d. settle

___c___ **10.** homogeneous
      a. uniform   c. different
      b. alone   d. separated

EXERCISE **3** Fill in the Blank

Use context clues to determine the word that best completes each sentence.

1. His access _____ to Blackbeard's treasure depended on his ability to unravel the code he found stuffed in the spine of an old book.

2. After learning that he had <u>inherited</u> his aunt's estate, Raymond began dreaming of ways to use his new fortune.

3. The doctor asked the patient some important lifestyle questions about exercise, alcohol use, smoking, and dietary habits, as well as about family <u>longevity</u> to determine the age of his parents and grandparents.

4. The upscale houses were very expensive, so marketing compaigns were aimed at individuals in a high <u>socio-economic</u> level.

5. In <u>previous</u> novels, the author always made the villain an obviously evil character; however, in her latest book, she created a new character who was difficult to recognize as either completely good or bad.

6. Third-world countries benefit from <u>contraception</u> methods to control the population, proper health care education, and better sanitary conditions that include clean water.

7. In an effort to <u>counteract</u> the rising numbers of mosquitoes carrying the West Nile virus, health officials recommend maintaining good drainage as well as emptying containers and pools that hold standing water.

8. Students in the chemistry lab collaborated on the project to <u>analyze</u> the test results and then report on their findings.

9. Instead of creating a <u>homogenous</u> group of individuals of similar age, the tour director paired a teenager with an elderly person so that each could offer his or her view of the trip.

10. Some students at the College of William and Mary are currently participating in an archaeological dig at the recently discovered site of the original fort in Jamestown to learn more about the <u>culture</u> of the earlier settlers as well as the Native Americans of Chief Powhatan's tribe.

EXERCISE **4** Application

Using context clues, insert the vocabulary word in the appropriate blank. A part-of-speech clue is given for each vocabulary word.

Angelo, one of the Lost Boys of Sudan, stopped by my office today. Taller than most of the students on campus, he has the moves of a slender, graceful basketball player. He once explained that he had **(1)** (v.) <u>inherit(ed)</u> his height from his parents who were also very tall, but then he explained that most of the natives of his country shared this trait.

During **(2)** (adj.) <u>previous</u> conferences, I would help Angelo **(3)** (v.) <u>analyze</u> some of the errors in his essays. "I want to do well in my studies," he explained, "so I can help my people have **(4)** (n.) <u>access</u> to a better life."

Angelo has many concerns for the people of his tribe. When he was a young boy, he saw his village destroyed and his family members killed. He was forced at the age of ten to travel hundreds of miles on foot with other refugees from his village. Because of their low **(5)** (adj.) <u>socio-economic</u> level, many of the villagers did not have a strong voice to get government help. Although they remained a close-knit group, they were hardly **(6)** (adj.) <u>homogenous</u>. There were men, women, and children of many ages and many talents. Those differences, however, did not matter.

Lately, Angelo has been selling bracelets woven with beads to raise money for his village. He wants to help improve living standards without making major changes to their **(7)** (n.) <u>culture</u> and their way of life. By sending money back home, he hopes to improve the **(8)** (n.) <u>longevity</u> of his people by providing funds for medical supplies. He also hopes to raise money to build a clinic and a school. He recognizes the importance of education and he feels medical personnel could inform his villagers about sanitation, good nutrition, and even **(9)** (n.) <u>contraception</u> to prevent overpopulation.

"If we can **(10)** (v.) <u>counteract</u> the effects of the war," Angelo says, "we can plant seeds of hope that will lead to a harvest of peace."

Stop and Think

 Choose any six words from the list and draw a picture representing each word. Do not label the pictures. Next, pair up, and give your partner 2 minutes to guess each vocabulary word you have represented in your drawings. (Answers will vary.)

Go to **www.etymonline.com** and research the origins and meanings of the following words:

1. *access:* From the Latin word *accessus*, which means "a coming to, an approach," the word *access* appeared in 1325 to mean "an attack of fever." Later in 1382, it meant "habit or power of getting into the presence of someone or something." The word was not used as a verb until 1962.

2. *culture:* In 1440, the word *culture* had evolved from the Latin word *cultura,* which was related to the terms *tend, guard, cultivate,* and *till*. During this time, it meant "tilling of the land." It was used to refer to education around 1510, and then later in 1805, the word referred to "the intellectual side of civilization." A few years later in 1867, it meant the "collective customs and achievements of a people." The terms "culture vulture" and "culture shock" appeared in the 1940s.

3. *homogeneous:* Originally from the Greek words *homos*, which means "same," and *genos*, which means "kind, gender," the word first appeared around 1641. In reference to milk, it appeared in England about 1883.

4. *inherit:* From the Latin *in*, which means "in" and *hereditare*, which means "to inherit," the word *inherit* appeared in 1304 to mean "to make someone an heir." Around 1340, the word *inherit* made reference to "receive inheritance."

5. *longevity:* From the Latin word *longaevitas*, which means "great age, long life," the word *longevity* first appeared in English around 1615.

UNIT 2

Review Test
Chapters 3–6

1 Word Parts

Match the definitions in Column 2 to the word parts in Column 1.

Column 1

d	**1.** pre-	
g	**2.** ab-	
a	**3.** forc	
b	**4.** -ly	
j	**5.** inter-	
e	**6.** -ate	
f	**7.** com-	
h	**8.** -tion	
i	**9.** -or	
c	**10.** de-	

Column 2

a. strong

b. in a certain manner

c. down; from; away

d. before

e. cause to become

f. with; together

g. away

h. condition

i. one who

j. between

2 Fill in the Blank

Use context clues to determine the best word from the box to complete each sentence.

access	immune	invasive	obtain	quest
anxiety	inherit	nutrient	prompt	scarce

1. Freshman year is the beginning of a <u>quest</u> to achieve the goal of a college degree and prepare for a successful career.

2

2. A few words of appreciation from a supervisor can <u>prompt</u> an employee to work harder and more efficiently.

3. Government employees are required to change their computer passwords every six months to ensure hackers cannot gain <u>access</u> to sensitive computer documents.

4. Mike realized that to <u>obtain</u> a job with an international shipping firm, he would need to take a foreign language and improve his ability to communicate with people from other countries.

5. To avoid a vitamin deficiency, people often take a supplement, especially if they do not eat enough fruits or vegetables to provide <u>nutrients</u>.

6. In some countries, paper is so <u>scarce</u> that students use all available space on a scrap before discarding it.

7. Many famous, talented people develop <u>anxiety</u> before a performance, but if they are well prepared, they overcome their fears once they are onstage.

8. "We must take care of our natural resources," warned Senator Bigley, "or our children will <u>inherit</u> a world of broken pieces."

9. Parents are urged to have their children's shots up to date to help them be <u>immune</u> to some diseases.

10. An <u>invasive</u> surgery such as a complicated heart bypass usually requires several weeks of recovery as well as a change of lifestyle afterward.

3 Book Connection

Use context clues to determine the best word from the box to complete each sentence.

alleviate	consumption	counteract	enhance	intervention
analyze	contaminate	culture	immune	vital

THE RADIOACTIVE BOY SCOUT

"Have you read this?" Marc asked as he held up a copy of *The Radioactive Boy Scout* by Ken Silverstein. "It's good reading for students who plan to major in chemistry or at least for those who want to **(1)** (v.) enhance _____ their background knowledge before they take a science course," he added.

Yelena **(2)** (v.) analyz(ed) _____ the cover, which seemed to glow with vibrant orange and green. "Tell me about it," she said.

Marc continued to explain that the nonfiction story was about a Michigan teenager whose principal goal was to own all of the elements of the periodic table and eventually build a nuclear breeder reactor in his parents' potting shed. Although the student had an amazing cognitive ability and talent and brilliance for science that many scientists would envy, David Hahn made barely passing grades and had almost no spelling aptitude, and had difficulty fitting into the **(3)** (n.) culture _____ of his school. Also, in spite of a scientific intellect, he had complete disregard for his own personal safety as he gathered radioactive material from everyday items such as smoke detectors and camping lanterns. He seemed to think he was **(4)** (adj.) immune _____ to the dangers of radiation. In some cases, he found material in the glow-in-the-dark faces of old clocks. Due to the **(5)** (n.) consumption _____ of radioactive particles from factory workers who would lick the tips of their brushes as they were painting the clock faces, such items were now only available in antique stores.

As Hahn grew more successful in the creation of a homemade nuclear breeder, he also realized his experiment was out of control. Therefore, he consulted another classmate—also self-taught in nuclear science—to determine how to **(6)** (v.) counteract _____ the effects of his new creation so he would not **(7)** (v.) contaminate _____ the entire city of Detroit, Michigan. The **(8)** (n.) intervention _____ of the federal government is the only thing

2

that prevented Hahn from damaging the neighborhood and causing destruction of his own **(9)** (adj.) vital_____ organs.

   The Radioactive Boy Scout is a true story about a young man's quest to achieve scientific stardom as well as a desire to **(10)** (v.) alleviate_____ the country's reliance on gas or oil for power. The book also provides an interesting look into the history of nuclear energy—the discoveries, the obstacles, and the reasons for the regulations.

4 Visual Connection

Write a caption for this picture using the words from the box. (Answers will vary.)

culture	imperative	pristine	significant	quench

George Pongratz

_____

_____

_____

_____

_____

_____

_____

5 Analogies

Choose the word that best completes the analogy.

1. dynamite : explosion :: laughter : ___a___
   a. catharsis   b. gift of gab   c. status

2. limb : trunk :: arms : ___b___
   a. catharsis   b. torso   c. culture

3. journey : road :: career path : ___c___
   a. investigator   b. status   c. alternative

4. silence : mute :: plan : ___c___
   a. culture   b. modeling   c. procedure

5. car : dent :: wall : ___a___
   a. recess   b. torso   c. culture

6. military : rank :: income : ___c___
   a. investigator   b. recess   c. status

7. psychic : fortune :: doctor : ___a___
   a. prognosis   b. recess   c. torso

8. passengers : airplanes :: diseases : ___b___
   a. prognosis   b. pathogens   c. intervention

9. geology : earth's crust :: anthropology : ___a___
   a. culture   b. recess   c. torso

10. artist : draw :: scientist : ___b___
   a. recess   b. analyze   c. investigator

UNIT **3** Vocabulary in
Social Sciences

CHAPTER
7

Vocabulary and
Psychology

Get **Ready** to **Read** About Psychology

Psychology is the study of mental processes and behavior. The word
psychology comes from the root *psych*, which means *mind* and the suffix
-ology, which means *study* or *science of*. As you read about psychology, you
will make connections to your own experiences, and you will grow to understand yourself and others better.

In this lesson, you will also draw on information you learned in
Chapter 1 about the word parts below.

1. The prefix *con-* means <u>with; together</u>.

2. The prefix *re-* means <u>again</u>.

3. The suffix *–ment* means *action* or *process* and usually indicates a noun.

acute	cope	inclination	overwhelm	resentment
contend	denial	jag	phase	wane

THE STAGES OF GRIEF

Grief is a natural and healthy response to our loss of something or someone. Elizabeth Kübler-Ross explains in her book *On Death and Dying* that grief occurs in stages, and she **contends** that understanding those stages helps us **cope** with our grief. According to Kübler-Ross, grief has five stages. The first stage of grief is *denial*. At first, we have an **inclination** to refuse to accept the reality of the loss. Denial protects us from the shock of the loss until we are better able to cope. The second stage is *anger*. Anger results from feeling abandoned or helpless. Sometimes **resentment** toward God or the one we lost takes first place in our emotions. The third **phase** is the *bargaining* phase. We may spend much time thinking about what we could have done differently to prevent the loss. The fourth phase is *depression*. Once we realize the depth of the loss, we often find we have trouble sleeping and concentrating. Frequent crying **jags** and feelings of loneliness, emptiness, isolation, and self-pity **overwhelm** us. The fifth and final stage of grief is *acceptance*. The **acute** pain of grief **wanes**, and we begin to make plans for our future. We learn to accept the new and different life that lies before us.

—Adapted from D.J. Henry, *The Skilled Reader*, p. 265.

VISUAL VOCABULARY

The full moon will begin to ___b___ until it will be barely visible, and then it will begin to grow full again.

a. contend
b. wane

Courtesy of Microsoft.

EXERCISE 🔳 Context Clues

Refer to the previous passage and use context clues from the sentences below to determine the definition of each of the following words in **bold** print. Do not consult a dictionary.

1. acute (ə-kyo͞ot′) adj.
   Because of its **acute** vision, the bald eagle, our national bird, can detect its prey from an altitude of 1,000 feet.

   ___d___ **Acute** means
   - a. alone.
   - b. dangerous.
   - c. inaccurate.
   - d. sharp.

2. contend (kən-tĕnd′) v.
   Scientists **contend** that stem cell research could eliminate diseases such as Alzheimer's and diabetes.

   ___c___ **Contend** means
   - a. disagree.
   - b. challenge.
   - c. state to be true.
   - d. abandon.

3. cope (kōp) v.
   People who enjoy the challenge of solving a problem and overcoming obstacles tend to **cope** well when they have to handle things in their lives that do not go according to their original plan.

   ___a___ **Cope** means
   - a. manage.
   - b. disrespect.
   - c. disapprove.
   - d. neglect.

4. denial (dĭ-nī′əl) n.
   Sometimes silence is a more effective response to a person's lie, while a loud **denial** may draw even more attention to a problem.

   ___a___ **Denial** means
   - a. refusal.
   - b. agreement.
   - c. surrender.
   - d. cooperation.

5. inclination (ĭn′klə-nā′shən) n
   "While I have an **inclination** to accept your invitation, I must refuse it since I need to study for my chemistry exam before I can go to the movies," Emily wrote in an e-mail to her lab partner.

   ___d___ **Inclination** means
   - a. independence.
   - b. disrespect.
   - c. sadness.
   - d. tendency.

6. jag (jăg) n.

Whenever she is nervous, my aunt begins a talking **jag**, chattering nonstop so that no one can interrupt.

_____b_____ **Jag** means

    a. push.   c. pain.

    b. spree.   d. tenderness.

7. phase (fāz) n.

The doctor explained that beginning around 12 months of age, children enter a **phase** in which they need to be gently disciplined as soon as they have done something wrong, as they are beginning to learn about cause and effect.

_____b_____ **Phase** means

    a. whole.   c. center.

    b. stage.   d. definition.

8. overwhelm (ōvər-hwĕlm′) v.

While the beginning of a semester seems easy at first to many freshmen, the papers, tests, and deadlines **overwhelm** many students at midterm time.

_____c_____ **Overwhelm** means

    a. bore.   c. upset.

    b. expect.   d. soothe.

9. resentment (rĭ-zĕnt′mənt) n.

After years of **resentment** because of the special treatment his brother received from their parents, Adam finally expressed his anger over having to do the work of two without being given any reward.

_____c_____ **Resentment** means

    a. happiness.   c. displeasure.

    b. contentment.   d. good will.

10. wane (wān) v.

Anthony's enthusiasm for tennis quickly **waned** when he realized he could not hit the ball with the racket.

_____b_____ **Wane** means

    a. increase.   c. recover.

    b. decrease.   d. compare.

EXERCISE 2 Word Sorts

Synonyms

Match the word to the synonyms or definitions that follow each blank.

1. wane _____ diminish; decline; decrease; lessen

2. phase _____ period; stage; position; step

3. acute _____ clever; keen; sharp; insightful

4. jag _____ binge; spree; fling; overindulgence

5. contend _____ argue; affirm; claim; assert

Antonyms

Select the letter of the word with the opposite meaning.

__a__ 6. resentment
    a. contentment   c. disgust
    b. anger   d. statement

__b__ 7. overwhelm
    a. confuse   c. direct
    b. bore   d. determine

__c__ 8. denial
    a. anger   c. confession
    b. expression   d. disease

__d__ 9. cope
    a. manage   c. surprise
    b. realize   d. mismanage

__a__ 10. inclination
    a. reluctance   c. dream
    b. tendency   d. depression

EXERCISE 3 Fill in the Blank

Use context clues to determine the word that best completes each sentence.

1. We grew worried about Anna as she became depressed after the break-up with her boyfriend, slipping into crying jag(s) _____ that would last for several hours, so we finally encouraged her to seek help at the campus counseling center.

2. Because of a bipolar disorder, Kaye Gibbons wrote her first book *Ellen Foster* in six weeks while she was in her manic <u>phase</u>, which is a period marked by extreme "highs" and boundless energy.

3. Some people <u>contend</u> that you must read a daily newspaper and a weekly news magazine to be a well-informed citizen.

4. While her husband was in office, it was reported that Barbara Bush asked family members to exchange only one Christmas present each in order to preserve their holiday traditions and not allow it to <u>overwhelm</u> everyone.

5. Although Einstein's <u>acute</u> intellect dazzled the world once he reached his mid-twenties, many are surprised to learn that he was an ordinary student in the primary grades and could be considered a late bloomer.

6. Some people have an <u>inclination</u> to interpret art before they develop a background knowledge of the artist, and as a result, they may miss the deeper meaning presented in a work.

7. In spite of the defendant's passionate <u>denial</u> of any wrongdoing, the jury found her guilty.

8. Instead of developing <u>resentment</u> over not being able to finish her education because of a lack of money, Alexis sought the guidance of the financial aid officer to help her determine new options for paying tuition.

9. Students who join a learning community on campus report greater success because of the support they receive in learning to <u>cope</u> with personal problems and managing academic challenges.

10. The trailers for the new film hinted that it would be another blockbuster; however, when word traveled that the movie was a disappointment, the ticket sales <u>wane(d)</u>.

EXERCISE 4 Application

Using context clues, insert the vocabulary word in the appropriate blank. A part-of-speech clue is given for each vocabulary word.

When many freshmen begin college, they find the experience **(1)** (v.) <u>overwhelm(s)</u> them because of new procedures, new surroundings, new friends, and new subjects in which they may lack background knowledge. Because many students are unsure how to

(2) (v.) cope _____ at first, they must find ways to manage these challenges. Educators **(3)** (v.) contend _____ that if freshmen follow a few strategies, their first-year college experience will be rewarding. First, they should consider the first weeks of school as a learning **(4)** (n.) phase _____, or stage of college in which they should listen to suggestions and be willing to follow the advice of successful students. For example, since many freshman have an **(5)** (adj.) inclination _____ to waste hours partying or instant messaging friends, they need to learn to manage their time and plan to study effectively about two hours outside of class for every one hour spent in a lecture or a lab. Second, instead of building **(6)** (n.) resentment _____ and frustration over the volumes of reading, writing, and studying now required of them, they should view assignments as learning opportunities and work on each one a little bit at a time. Third, when enthusiasm for a course **(7)** (v.) wane(s) _____, students should find some ways to make studying more enjoyable. For instance, they could join a study group, volunteer for a campus project that has a connection to the course, or seek the advice of the instructor. In addition, some students can develop an **(8)** (adj.) acute _____ sense of isolation during that first semester, and a sharp and painful loneliness will prevent good concentration. Therefore, they should make time for extra-curricular activities to connect with others. **(9)** (n.) Denial _____ of a problem only makes it grow, so they need to remember that college is a community and they are an important part that makes it run smoothly. Finally, they should recognize that nothing good happens fast, and moving information from short-term memory to working memory and then to long-term memory takes rehearsal and practice. By reviewing their notes every day for just a few minutes, they will avoid crying **(10)** (n.) jag(s) _____ at the end of the semester when they are studying all night and losing important hours of sleep. By following these guidelines, many students will look back on their first-year college experience as a rewarding, successful time of growth.

Stop and Think

 Use a highlighter to color in the circles next to the words you can define without looking at the definitions, and then pair up with a classmate to share your answers.

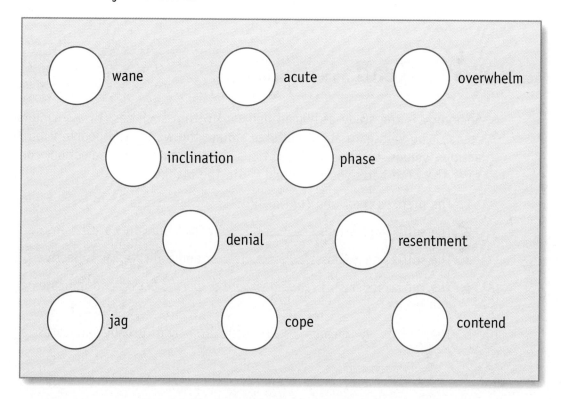

 Go to **http://www.npr.org/templates/story/story.php?storyId=3871067** and listen to the excerpt about the death of Elizabeth Kübler-Ross, the pioneer who introduced the idea of the stages of grief. In a paragraph, summarize your opinion of the radio clip from "Talk of the Nation" on National Public Radio and use at least four vocabulary words from this chapter. (Answers will vary.)

8

Vocabulary and Sociology

Get Ready to Read About Sociology

Sociology is the study of human behavior within societies. In a sociology course, you will learn about cultures around the world, and people's inter-actions, values, customs, and traditions. Before you read the selection, con-sider the word parts you know and fill in the blanks.

1. The prefixes *com-* and *con-* mean _with, or together_.

2. The suffix *-ate* means _cause to become_ and indicates a _verb_.

3. The suffix *-ful* means _full of_ and indicates an adjective.

4. The suffix *-ive* means *tending toward a specific action* and indicates an adjective.

5. The suffix *-ly* means _like or resembling_ and usually indicates an _adverb_.

| candid | consequently | diligent | motivate | strive |
| competitive | decisive | genial | sibling | tactful |

BIRTH ORDER AND
PERSONALITY TRAITS

Some experts believe that birth order—the family position into which we are born—leads to many of our other traits. Whether we are the oldest, the youngest, or the middle child among **siblings**, the order in which we are born can influence both the kinds of goals we set and the ways we relate to other people. Understanding the effect of birth order may help us better understand others and ourselves.

Being born first often results in leadership skills. Only children are also included in this group. Firstborns are often **competitive**, **diligent**, and high-achieving. **Consequently**, many firstborns earn degrees in higher education and become leaders in large corporations. People in this group often **strive** for perfection. They tend to be responsible, organized, and **decisive**.

Middle children, by contrast, are often known as peacemakers. They can see both sides of an issue and find the places where people can agree. Middle children are good managers and leaders. People in this group are often flexible, **genial,** and generous. They are often **tactful** even though they can be competitive. Being the middle child results in a person who is balanced and skilled at getting along with others.

Because of their position in the family, youngest children often love to be around people. The baby of the family is likely to be outgoing and fun-loving. Youngest children are direct and **candid.** Many youngest children become highly successful salespeople as a result of their ability to **motivate** others. In summary, birth order seems to have a strong effect on a person's nature.

—Adapted from D.J. Henry, *The Skilled Reader*, p. 356.

VISUAL VOCABULARY

This ___b___ group of soccer players probably has a close, friendly connection that will help them cooperate as a team.

a. decisive
b. genial

Courtesy of Microsoft.

EXERCISE **1** Context Clues

Refer to the previous passage and use context clues from the sentences below to determine the definition of each of the following words in **bold** print. Do not consult a dictionary.

1. candid (kăn′dĭd) adj.
A **candid** answer from a true friend is worth more than dishonest praise from an acquaintance.

___d___ **Candid** means
a. dishonest.   c. reasonable.
b. unfair.   d. honest.

2. competitive (kəm-pĕt′ĭ-tĭv) adj.
Because of his keenly **competitive** nature, Nick made a contest of even the smallest events to create a ready-for-action mood in his friends.

___c___ **Competitive** means
a. numbness.   c. spirited.
b. suspicion.   d. sadness.

3. consequently (kŏn′sĭ-kwĕnt′lē) adv.
The Beaufort scale is a descriptive list of various wind speeds; **consequently**, sailors should always refer to it when considering the safety of a voyage.

___b___ **Consequently** means
a. before.   c. first.
b. therefore.   d. when.

4. decisive (dĭ-sī′sĭv) adj.
   During Laurie's senior year of college, she became **decisive** about her future when she finalized her plans to volunteer for the Peace Corps to teach life skills to young women in West Africa.

   __b__ **Decisive** means

a. insignificant.	c. uncertain.
b. determined.	d. bored.

5. diligent (dĭl′ə-jənt) adj.
   One of the most **diligent** students in art class, Nate would spend hours in the college studio late into the night, working hard to perfect the details of his sculptures.

   __a__ **Diligent** means

a. hard-working.	c. lonely.
b. lazy.	d. careless.

6. genial (jĭ-nī′əl) adj.
   Although he appeared **genial** and good-natured, Adam's personality changed completely when he was in the courtroom heartlessly defending his client.

   __c__ **Genial** means

a. harsh.	c. friendly.
b. mean.	d. slowly.

7. motivate (mō′tə-vāt′) v.
   Some music can **motivate** a person to concentrate better, exercise longer, or work faster.

   __a__ **Motivate** means

a. inspire.	c. ease.
b. depress.	d. stretch.

8. sibling (sĭb′lĭng) n.
   With four **siblings**, Justin had to learn cooperation and peacemaking skills early, so learning to get along in the freshman dorm was easy for him.

   __d__ **Sibling** means

a. mother.	c. relative.
b. father.	d. brother or sister.

9. strive (strīv) v.

Our teacher explained that we should view our mistakes as lessons and **strive** to learn from them without repeating them, so that every day we become a better version of ourselves.

___d___ **Strive** means

 a. look down on.   c. surrender.
 b. surprise.   d. try hard.

10. tactful (tăkt′fəl) adj.

Molly's doctor chose her words carefully and in a **tactful** way explained that she needed to lose 30 pounds to lead a more healthful lifestyle.

___c___ Tactful means

 a. cruel.   c. thoughtful.
 b. disrespectful.   d. alert.

EXERCISE 2 Word Sorts

Synonyms

Match the word to the synonyms or definitions that follow each blank.

1. competitive _____ rivaling; vying; ambitious; opposing

2. sibling _____ brother; sister

3. strive _____ try hard; attempt; work; aim

4. decisive _____ sure; certain; firm; conclusive

5. consequently _____ accordingly; then; therefore; hence

Antonyms

Select the letter of the word(s) with the opposite meaning.

___a___ **6.** diligent

 a. slack   c. active
 b. hardworking   d. silent

___b___ **7.** candid

 a. forthright   c. obvious
 b. insincere   d. imperfect

___b___ **8.** genial

 a. friendly   c. silent
 b. mean   d. careful

_a_ **9.** motivate
    a. paralyze   c. pursue
    b. excite   d. move

_d_ **10.** tactful
    a. thoughtful   c. sly
    b. careful   d. rude

EXERCISE **3** Fill in the Blank

Use context clues to determine the word that best completes each sentence.

1. A _genial_ person, Adam usually attracted people because they were drawn to his friendly, upbeat personality.

2. The salesman showed us the old, used car within our price range, and in a _tactful_ manner explained that the car was an economical, pre-owned vehicle.

3. I have only one _sibling_, but my sister has also been my best friend.

4. Students who _strive_ to focus on understanding are more successful in their academics than those who just try to memorize facts before a test.

5. Lance Armstrong's book, _It's Not About the Bike_, has _motivate(d)_ many young athletes to continue working in spite of difficult odds.

6. One of the most _candid_ and brutally honest comments Johnny Depp ever made was when he said, "I think everybody's nuts."

7. Researchers who have been studying the brains of babies recently concluded that infants can feel jealousy and _consequently_ will cry simply to get attention.

8. Annette confidently walked up to the voting booth, and with a _decisive_ air, made her selection for governor after having made a definite decision following the televised debate.

9. The two colleges showed their _competitive_ spirit as each side tried to outdo the other in making noise.

10. The _diligent_ doctor was known for his careful, painstaking examinations before making a final diagnosis.

EXERCISE 4 Application

Using context clues, insert the vocabulary word in the appropriate blank. A part-of-speech clue is given for each vocabulary word.

For years scientists have been studying what **(1)** (v.) motivate(s) some people to become successful. Some researchers believe that children can demonstrate signs of giftedness at a very early age. Others, however, point to someone like Albert Einstein who was 4 years old before he could speak and 7 years old before he could read. Likewise some children are **(2)** (adj.) competitive long before they begin school, and they **(3)** (v.) strive to be first in everything they try. Is it because successful people are more **(4)** (adj.) diligent and hard working? That is a possibility, especially if you consider Colonel Sanders who was rejected more than a thousand times before someone was willing to take a chance on his chicken recipe, which eventually led to his KFC empire. Family connections and **(5)** (n.) sibling support are sometimes considered helpful. For example, even though teachers told Thomas Edison that he was too stupid to learn anything, his mother's **(6)** (adj.) decisive move to teach him at home proved them wrong, a decision that would eventually have an impact on the world with the invention of the incandescent light.

Often failure comes before success. For instance, the friendly and **(7)** (adj.) genial Walt Disney was fired by a **(8)** (adj.) candid newspaper editor who told him with brutal honesty that he had "no good ideas." While the editor's comment was not **(9)** (adj.) tactful, Disney proved him wrong and built his own business in spite of the insult. Many more stories exist of people who overcame the cruel comments of others; **(10)** (adv.) <u>consequently</u>, their success resulted from hard work, talent, passion for their craft, and many, many hours of practice.

—Adapted from Beebe, Beebe, & Redmond, *Interpersonal Communication: Relating to Others*, 3rd ed., p. 50.

Stop and Think

 Using at least one vocabulary word from this chapter, create a pyramid summary of the sociology selection on birth order. (Answers will vary, but a sample is provided.)

<u>Birth order</u>

<u>may affect personality traits,</u>

<u>so that firstborns are competitive,</u>

<u>middle children are peacemaking leaders,</u>

<u>while the youngest children are fun and outgoing.</u>

 Go to **www.etymonline.com** and research the origins of the following words:

1. candid <u>From the Latin word *candidum* that means "white, pure, sincere," the word *candid* appeared in English in 1630. In 1675 it was used to mean "frank, honest."</u>

2. genial <u>In 1746 the word *genial* was used to mean "cheerful, friendly" from the Latin. It is related to the Latin word *genius* that means "guardian spirit."</u>

3. sibling <u>From the old English word *sibling*, the word meant "relative kinsman." In 1500 the word *sib* was used in Scotland. Today it means "brother or sister."</u>

Vocabulary and American Government

Get Ready to Read About American Government

To fulfill general education requirements, some college students take a class about government. These courses often provide a historical background and the cause-and-effect relationship of current events and laws. To do well in such a class, you will want to read a daily newspaper and keep up with information in a weekly news magazine. In addition, you should recognize that words in this subject area have multiple meanings, often focusing on legislation—both the laws and the lawmakers.

Before you read the selection, consider the word parts you know and fill in the blanks here.

1. The prefix *com-* means <u>with, together</u>.

2. The prefix *dis-* means <u>not, separated from</u>.

3. The suffix *–ity* means <u>quality, trait</u> and usually indicates a <u>noun</u>.

4. The suffix *–ize* means <u>make, do, cause to become</u> and usually indicates a <u>verb</u>.

boycott	displace	mobilize	policy	provision
compose	migrant	plight	probability	tactic

CIVIL RIGHTS AND PUBLIC POLICY

Hispanic Americans (or Latinos, as some prefer to be called)—chiefly from Mexico, Puerto Rico, and Cuba but also from El Salvador, Honduras, and other countries in Central America—will soon **displace** African Americans as the largest minority group. Today they **compose** about 10 percent of the U.S. population.

The first major efforts on behalf of civil rights for Hispanics date only from the mid-1960s. Hispanic leaders drew from the **tactics** of the African-American civil rights movement and sit-ins, **boycotts,** marches, and related activities to draw attention to their cause. Inspired by the NAACP's Legal Defense Fund, they also created the Mexican American Legal Defense and Education Fund (MALDEF) in 1968 to help argue their cause in court. In addition, Hispanic groups began **mobilizing** in other ways to protect their interests. An early prominent example was the United Farm Workers, led by Cesar Chavez, who publicized the **plight** of **migrant** workers, a large proportion of whom are Hispanic.

Like Native Americans, Hispanic Americans benefit from the nondiscrimination policies originally passed to protect African Americans. **Provisions** of the Voting Rights Act of 1965 covered San Antonio, Texas, and thereby permitted Hispanic voters to lend weight to the election of Mayor Henry Cisneros. There are now about 6,000 elected Hispanic officials in the United States, and Hispanic-Americans play a prominent role in the politics of such major cities as Houston, Miami, Los Angeles, and San Diego. In 1973, Hispanics won a victory when the Supreme Court found that multimember electoral districts (in which more than one person represents a single district) in Texas discriminated against minority groups because they decrease the **probability** of a minority being elected. Nevertheless, poverty, discrimination, and language barriers continue to depress Hispanic voter registration and turnout.

—"Civil Rights and Public Policy" from Edwards, George C., III,
Martin P. Wattenberg, Robert L. Lineberry,
Government in America, 9th ed. Longman, 2000. p. 157.

VISUAL VOCABULARY

After a college student graduates and begins learning more about his new career,

each day will also be ___a___ of learning to do housework and how to cook in order to save money.

  a. composed
  b. displaced

George Pongratz

EXERCISE 1 Context Clues

Refer to the previous passage and use context clues from the sentences below to determine the definition of each of the following words in **bold** print. Do not consult a dictionary.

1. boycott (boi'kŏt') n.
When the quality and selection of the college cafeteria food began to worsen, the students planned a **boycott** and bought their food at the convenience foods section of a local grocery store instead.

___c___ **Boycott** means
  a. improvement.   c. ban.
  b. approval.   d. support.

2. compose (kəm-pōz') v.
Our college population is **composed** of in-state as well as out-of-state students, which makes it an interesting mixture of people from many localities.

___a___ **Compose** means
  a. make up.   c. ruin.
  b. unsettle.   d. disorganize.

3. displace (dĭs-plās) v.

Following the apartment fire that **displaced** several families, the Red Cross stepped in to offer support and find new temporary housing for those who had lost their homes.

__b__ **Displace** means

    a. settle.
    b. uproot.
    c. appoint.
    d. include.

4. migrant (mī′grənt) adj.

The Grapes of Wrath, a prize-winning novel by John Steinbeck, tells the story of the Joads and other **migrant** families traveling across the United States in search of a better life during the Depression.

__b__ **Migrant** means

    a. wealthy.
    b. traveling.
    c. powerful.
    d. happy.

5. mobilize (mō′bə-līz′) v.

After looking at the clutter, Alisha **mobilized** the entire family to quickly clean and rearrange furniture before their weekend guests arrived in a few days.

__d__ **Mobilize** means

    a. turn off.
    b. debate.
    c. stop.
    d. move into action.

6. plight (plīt) n.

Some government organizations are now sponsoring workshops for area bankers and retailers to help them realize the **plight** of those living in poverty—especially the difficulties they face when transportation is a barrier to keeping a job or their services are cut off.

__c__ **Plight** means

    a. pleasure.
    b. interest.
    c. difficulty.
    d. ease.

7. policy (pŏl′ĭ-sē) n.

Derrick was frustrated when he received a ticket for parking on the line in a space on campus—especially when he complained and was told, "That is our college's **policy**."

__d__ **Policy** means

    a. presentation.
    b. problem.
    c. performance.
    d. agreed practice.

8. probability (prŏb′ə-bĭl′ĭ-tē) n.
   The **probability** of snow did not prevent Amy from working on her project, which was due the next day.

   ___a___ **Probability** means
       a. likelihood.   c. service.
       b. impossibility   d. job.

9. provision (prə-vĭzh′ən) n.
   A **provision** in the celebrities' prenuptial agreement stated that if the couple divorced, the wife would receive only the Z4 convertible in the settlement, since that was originally her car anyway.

   ___c___ **Provision** means
       a. movement.   c. condition.
       b. entrance.   d. rejection.

10. tactic (tăk′tĭk) n.
    To organize his essay better, Aaron used the **tactic** of first creating a concept map and then an outline—a strategy he had learned from his tutor in the writing center.

    ___a___ **Tactic** means
        a. plan for reaching a goal.   c. settlement in a disagreement.
        b. order for merchandise.   d. avoidance of a problem.

EXERCISE 2 Word Sorts

Synonyms

Match the word to the synonyms or definitions that follow each blank.

1. compose _____ construct; go in; form; make up

2. tactic _____ plan; strategy; method; means

3. policy _____ guideline; practice; code; administration

4. probability _____ chance; anticipation; expectation; likelihood

5. plight _____ trouble; difficulty; dilemma; bad news

Antonyms

Select the letter of the word(s) with the opposite meaning.

__d__ **6.** migrant
a. moving   c. foreign
b. visiting   d. stationary

__a__ **7.** boycott
a. support   c. discouragement
b. ban   d. disapproval

__d__ **8.** mobilize
a. motivate   c. symbolize
b. free   d. paralyze

__b__ **9.** provision
a. code   c. plan
b. rejection   d. agreement

__a__ **10.** displace
a. put back   c. exile
b. remove   d. budge

EXERCISE **3** Fill in the Blank

Use context clues to determine the word that best completes each sentence.

1. In the film *Air Force One*, the vice-president asks the president why they cannot break from the country's _policy_____ of not negotiating with terrorists just this once, and he replies, "If you give a mouse a cookie."

2. As fighting increased in her village, Zoya, a young Afghan girl, and her grandmother flee the area and become _migrants_____ in search of safety at a refugee camp.

3. When he began college, Ben had enough money for only one year; nevertheless, this lack of funds _mobilize(d)_____ him to get a summer job and apply for scholarships to help finance the next year.

4. When the citizens of New London, Connecticut, complained about the city's plan to seize their property for the development of expensive condominiums, they pointed to the <u>provision</u> in the Fifth Amendment of the Constitution that states "nor shall private property be taken for public use, without just compensation."

5. Our student body is <u>compose(d)</u> of 7,000 full-time students—many of whom have part-time jobs.

6. The <u>probability</u> of rain can only be accurately predicted within a three-day period, which indicates the inaccuracy of a long-range forecast.

7. Learning to identify text frames, or writing patterns, is a good reading <u>tactic</u> for finding the main idea.

8. In the novel *The Samurai's Gardens* by Gail Tsukiyama, the <u>plight</u> of the people who get the skin disease known as leprosy is tenderly described.

9. In war-torn areas, many families are <u>displace(d)</u> from their homes and must find another place to live.

10. When the colonists' complaints about the British soldiers were ignored by the English king, the colonists joined in a <u>boycott</u> of imported goods—an event that led to the Boston Tea Party.

EXERCISE 4 Application

Using context clues, insert the vocabulary word in the appropriate blank. A part-of-speech clue is given for each vocabulary word.

Are you someone who thinks life is going to be good if you are willing to work harder? Many people do not understand how complicated the issue can be. For instance, the **(1)** (n.) <u>plight</u> of the **(2)** (adj.) <u>migrant</u> worker has not always been something that people accurately understood. Many of us have no concept of suffering or what it must be like to keep moving from place to place in search of a better, safer life for your family. Finding shelter after being **(3)** (v.) <u>displace(d)</u> and trying to **(4)** (v.) <u>mobilize</u> quickly when you realize your family is in danger can be frightening. Yet, there are people in the United States who **(5)** (v.) <u>compose</u> the population of good workers, help run the country, and complete construction projects who may have had such fears. In fact, the **(6)** (n.) <u>probability</u> that each of us has encountered someone who has faced such difficulty is very high.

On March 25, 2006, protestors gathered in Los Angeles, California, in front of City Hall to protest the federal immigration legislation. The **(7)** (n.) <u>tactic</u> has been used many times in the country to draw attention to a growing problem. Was it a **(8)** (n.) <u>boycott</u> of a popular retail chain? No, in this case, the problem was the need to make **(9)** (n.) <u>provisions</u> of legal status to the more than 11 million illegal immigrants. The impressive numbers of people gathered that day to express their desire that the government **(10)** (n.) <u>policy</u> be changed.

Stop and Think

 Visit **www.etymonline.com** and determine what words would best complete the following word histories.

1. boycott:

   In Ireland in 1880, a land agent named <u>Captain Charles Boycott</u> was punished for refusing to lower the <u>rent</u> for his tenant <u>farmers</u>. As a result, the <u>Irish Land League</u> kicked him out of their organization, thus causing the <u>newspapers</u> around the world to coin the new word *boycott*.

2. compose:

In <u>1475</u>, the <u>French</u> word *composer*, which means *put together, arrange*, came from the prefix *com-*, which means <u>with</u> and *poser*, which means <u>to place</u>. These originated from the Latin *ponere*, which means *to put, place*, as in the word *position*. The word *composed* used in the musical sense first appeared in <u>1597</u>. The use of composed with the meaning *calm* appeared in <u>1621</u>, and the word <u>composure</u> surfaced in 1667.

3. policy:

The word *policy* that refers to a *way of management* evolved from the <u>Old French</u> word *policie*, which meant *civil administration* in the 14th century. This came from the <u>Latin</u> term *politia* which means the *state*, which actually came from the <u>Greek</u> word *politeia*, meaning *state, administration, government*, and *citizenship*. The Greek word *polites* means *citizen* and the word *polis* means <u>city, state</u>. The term *policy*, as defined in this chapter, was first recorded around <u>1406</u>.

4. provision:

The word *provision*, as in *providing beforehand*, was first recorded in <u>1380</u> and originally referred to appointments that were made <u>before</u> a position was vacant. This word was from the Latin *provisio*, which means <u>foresight, preparation</u>. The meaning *supply of food* for the word *provision* was recorded in <u>1610</u>.

5. mobilize:

The word *mobilize* comes from the <u>French</u> word *mobiliser* in <u>1838</u>, which was formed from the word *mobile*, meaning *movable*. The military use of the word first appeared in <u>1853</u>.

Study the pictures below and decide which vocabulary word from this chapter best summarizes each image. Write the word, the definition, and your reason for choosing the word. (Answers may vary.)

Word	Definition	Reason
1. migrant		
2. tactic		
3. probability		
4. plight		
5. displace		

Vocabulary and Anthropology

Get Ready to Read About Anthropology

Anthropology is a combination of history and sociology that examines the origin of humans as well as their social and cultural development. The term is a combination of the root *anthrop*, which means *human*, and suffix *-ology*, which means *the study of*. In this chapter, you will read about a place that has fascinated historians for many years. Note the time is listed as B.C.E. (before common era).

Before you read, review some of the following word parts.

1. The prefix *circum-* means <u>around</u>.

2. The prefix *dis-* means *separated from* or *not*.

3. The prefix *in-* means <u>within; into</u>

4. The root *lith* means <u>stone</u>.

5. The root *magni* means <u>large</u>.

6. The root *neo* means <u>new</u>.

7. The root *sol* means *alone* or *sun*.

8. The suffix *–ant* means <u>one who</u> and indicates a <u>noun</u>.

9. The suffix *–ic* means *like, resembling, of,* and indicates an <u>adjective</u>.

10. The suffix *–ly* means <u>in the manner of, like</u> and indicates an <u>adverb</u>.

| bank | circumference | inhabitant | monument | solstice |
| cathedral | display | magnificently | Neolithic | zeal |

STONEHENGE

The wealth, political organization, learning, and religious **zeal** of Wessex were **displayed** even more **magnificently** in the great stone **monuments** its **inhabitants** built. The most impressive of these is Stonehenge, which rises boldly and mysteriously out of Salisbury Plain. Like a Gothic **cathedral,** Stonehenge was built over many centuries. Sometime between 2900 and 2500 B.C.E., the **Neolithic** people of Salisbury Plain built Stonehenge I. This was a great ditch with **banks** built up on both sides; it was 380 feet in **circumference,** with an avenue leading out of it. One hundred feet outside the circle, down the avenue, stood a great stone, now called the heel stone. Standing at the center of Stonehenge, one can see the midsummer sunrise, or summer **solstice,** over the heel stone. Within the ditch, there were once four stones that formed a rectangle that stood at right angles to the line of the midsummer sunrise.

—From Clayton Roberts, David Roberts, and Douglas Bisson, *A History of England*, v. 1, 4th ed., p. 10. Copyright© 2001. Published by Prentice Hall.

VISUAL VOCABULARY

Visitors to Stonehenge are no longer allowed near the huge stones, except around June 22nd, the summer ___b___, when people are permitted to gather to celebrate Midsummer's Day.

a. zeal
b. solstice

Elizabeth Pongratz

EXERCISE ■1 Context Clues

Refer to the previous passage and use context clues from the sentences below to determine the definition of each of the following words in **bold** print. Do not consult a dictionary.

1. bank (bănk) n.
We sat on the **bank** overlooking the river and watched the sun tint the sky purple and pink before it set.

_____d_____ **Bank** means

    a. money.
    b. sunset.

    c. wave.
    d. a steep natural incline.

2. cathedral (kə-thē′drəl) n.
Most of the **cathedrals** and churches in Western Europe are hundreds of years older than those in the United States.

_____a_____ **Cathedral** means

    a. large important church.
    b. graveyard.

    c. priest.
    d. old museum.

3. circumference (sər-kŭm′fər-əns) n.
When we measured the track's **circumference**—that is, the distance around—we discovered that it was longer than one-half mile.

_____a_____ **Circumference** means

    a. distance around.
    b. height.

    c. weight.
    d. depth.

4. display (dĭ-splā′) v.
Maurice was very humble about his accomplishments as an athlete, and he would not allow his family to **display** his awards and trophies.

_____b_____ **Display** means

    a. excel.
    b. exhibit or show.

    c. lose.
    d. practice.

5. inhabitant (ĭn-hăb′ĭ-tənt) n.
As soon as they arrived on the scene, the firefighters searched the burning dwelling for any **inhabitants** who needed to be rescued.

_____c_____ **Inhabitant** means

    a. hero.
    b. victim.

    c. resident.
    d. solution.

6. magnificently (măg-nĭf´ĭ-sənt-lē) adv.
The symphony played **magnificently** during the Labor Day concert, and everyone agreed they had never heard the music of *Star Wars* played so well.

___b___ **Magnificently** means
   a. in a poor manner.   c. in a weak manner.
   b. in a grand or noble manner.   d. in a negative way.

7. monument (mŏn´yə-mənt) n.
After climbing steps all week on our vacation, we decided to relax on the beach rather than visit one more **monument**.

___a___ **Monument** means
   a. building or structure that serves as a memorial.
   b. beach house.
   c. tall steps.
   d. vacation cottage.

8. Neolithic (nē´ə-lĭth´ĭk) adj.
In our history class, we learned that the **Neolithic** Age was a period in which humans began to use stone tools.

___d___ **Neolithic** means
   a. Bronze Age.
   b. period before man.
   c. period after machines were developed.
   d. New Stone Age.

9. solstice (sŏl´stĭs) n.
Every December, my friend Molly plans a celebration of the winter **solstice**, which is the longest night of the year.

___d___ **Solstice** means
   a. a healing power.
   b. a celebration.
   c. a time of solitary confinement.
   d. twice a year when the sun is the farthest from the equator.

10. zeal (zēl) n.
We always enjoy going to our biology class because Dr. Rabiero teaches with such earnestness and **zeal**.

___a___ **Zeal** means
   a. enthusiasm.   c. a good lesson.
   b. lack of energy.   d. a sensible plan.

EXERCISE 2 Word Sorts

Synonyms

Match the word to the synonyms or definitions that follow each blank.

1. <u>Neolithic</u> the New Stone Age; the period around 10,000 B.C.E. when agriculture developed as well as the use of stone tools.

2. <u>circumference</u> the boundary line of a circle; the distance around the circle

3. <u>monument</u> memorial; obelisk; a structure of remembrance; statue

4. <u>solstice</u> the two times a year when the sun is at the greatest distance of the equator

5. <u>bank</u> waterfront; cay; shore; piled mass of earth

Antonyms

Select the letter of the word(s) with the opposite meaning.

<u>d</u> 6. zeal
   a. passion   c. disappointment
   b. energy   d. boredom

<u>d</u> 7. magnificently
   a. slowly   c. politely
   b. grandly   d. poorly

<u>a</u> 8. inhabitant
   a. intruder   c. citizen
   b. resident   d. member

<u>c</u> 9. display
   a. advertise   c. hide
   b. arrange   d. beg

<u>c</u> 10. cathedral
   a. church   c. unholy place
   b. holy place   d. temple

EXERCISE **3** Fill in the Blank

Use context clues to determine the vocabulary word that best completes each sentence.

1. Marian said that *Anna Karenina* is one of the most <u>magnificently</u> written books of all time, so it is no surprise that the Russian novel is considered a classic.

2. We realized Adam's <u>zeal</u> for protecting animals had gone too far when he not only gave up red meat, fish, and poultry, but also most vegetables, which he said cry when they are harvested.

3. The <u>Neolithic</u> period was a time in which humans began forming communities, farming, and raising animals.

4. When Irene was first learning to drive, she accidentally overshot a ditch when she was making a U-turn, and she landed on the <u>bank</u> of someone's front lawn.

5. When he sailed to a small island near his neighborhood, Ben was surprised to discover a small tree house, with evidence of an <u>inhabitant</u> who had set up residence.

6. Doug led us to two rooms in which he <u>displayed</u> baseball uniforms, autographed pictures and balls, bats, letters, and other items that once belonged to professional baseball players.

7. While in Washington, D.C., we visited two <u>monuments</u>: the Lincoln Memorial and the Jefferson Memorial.

8. According to legend, if a woman captures the early morning dew of the summer <u>solstice</u> and pats it on her face, she will retain her youthful appearance.

9. The <u>cathedral</u> at Chartres, France, once served as a church, museum, concert hall, and meeting place.

10. When James was born, the nurse immediately weighed him and then measured his length as well as the <u>circumference</u> of his head.

EXERCISE 4 Application

Using context clues, insert the vocabulary word in the appropriate blank. A part-of-speech clue is given for each vocabulary word.

Wendy was nervous as she prepared a presentation that would be **(1)** (v.) display(ed)_____ for one of her architecture classes. The students were told to create a model of a structure. The trick, however, was that all of the materials had to be objects found on campus. This assignment was received with less **(2)** (n.) zeal_____ by the very rich students, who were used to buying whatever expensive materials they needed. Wendy, who had few resources, felt this new approach was more fair, and she was determined to create a **(3)** (adv.) magnificently_____ constructed model, one that would gain the respect of her professors and maybe earn her a summer internship.

First, she created a mossy **(4)** (n.) bank_____ along a ribbon of blue river. Next, she drew a circle and measured the **(5)** (n.) circumference_____, or the distance around, so that she could calculate the height and width of the structure. Wendy also decided the building would be a **(6)** (n.) monument_____ to honor the **(7)** (adj.) Neolithic_____ people who first found new ways to use stone as tools. Consequently, she decided to create a few **(8)** (n.) inhabitant(s)_____, nearby residents, to stand outside the building. This would help people get a better view of just how big a structure her model was scaled for.

The greatest challenge was yet to come, when Wendy considered what found materials to use for the actual building. The answer came to her in an unlikely place: the school cafeteria. While trying to cut her breakfast waffles, she discovered they were as hard as any granite. Aha! She quickly asked her friends to go back through the line and collect more stacks of waffles, which she then took back to her dorm room. For days she cut, glued, and shaped until her magnificent Gothic **(9)** (n.) <u>cathedral</u> with a steeple, arched windows, and gargoyles appeared. As a final touch, she positioned a prism inside the church's sanctuary to catch the light of the summer **(10)** (n.) <u>solstice</u> and sparkle through the windows.

Stop and Think

3-2-1

Write three sentences using three of the adjectives. (Answers will vary.)

_____

_____

_____

Write two sentences using two of the nouns.

_____

_____

Write one sentence using the verb.

_____

Go to **www.exn.ca/mysticplaces/construction.asp** and read about the construction of Stonehenge. In the space below, summarize what you discovered about the bluestone that was used to create the monument.

Transporting the heavy stones over a great distance would have been a challenge.

A new theory that most researchers do not accept yet, though, is that the bluestone

was available in the area because of glacial shifts.

Review Test
Chapters 7-10

1 Word Parts

Match the definitions in Column 2 with the word parts in Column 1.

Column 1

_d_ **1.** auto-

_f_ **2.** soph

_b_ **3.** in-

_h_ **4.** -ate

_i_ **5.** bio

_a_ **6.** circum-

_c_ **7.** neo-

_j_ **8.** graph

_g_ **9.** magni

_e_ **10.** phil

Column 2

a. around

b. within; into

c. new

d. self

e. love

f. wisdom

g. large

h. cause to become

i. life

j. write; draw

2 Fill in the Blank

Use context clues to determine the best word from the box to complete each sentence.

bank	compose	contend	decisive	migrant
circumference	consequently	cope	jag	Neolithic

1. Some physicists <u>contend</u> that a person could fall through a black hole and work his way out the other side.

2. Learning to <u>cope</u> with a chronic condition such as heart disease or diabetes requires a plan as well as the support and encouragement of family and friends.

3. Some behaviors, such as gambling and overeating, can be addictive; <u>consequently</u>, a person will develop cravings rather than the physical withdrawals experienced with drug addictions.

4. Not a <u>decisive</u> person, the *Peanuts* cartoon character Charlie Brown always had difficulty choosing a plan or making a decision.

5. Our government class is researching issues facing <u>migrant</u> workers from Mexico who have to get on a long waiting list to become naturalized citizens.

6. The courses that <u>compose</u> the new curriculum include chemistry, sociology, and ethics.

7. We sat on the <u>bank</u> of the river and watched the sun set.

8. Cindy goes on a cleaning <u>jag</u> twice a year, furiously scrubbing and organizing.

9. While exploring the canyon, we found a circular track with a <u>circumference</u> of 40 feet, and in the center we discovered huge boulders with puzzling carvings.

10. The art history class studied the <u>Neolithic</u> period, a time when many of the first stone statues represented humans or animals.

3

3 Book Connection

Use context clues to determine the best word from the box to complete each sentence.

denial	displayed	plight	sibling	tactic
diligent	magnificently	resentment	strive	wane

A CHILD CALLED "IT"

A Child Called "It" by David Pelzer is the first book in a series of autobiographical accounts about the bold attempts of a young boy to survive in spite of the abuse **(1)** (v.) display_____(ed) by his mother. Curiously, Pelzer's **(2)** (n.) sibling(s)_____ are never the recipients of the same mistreatment he has to endure, which is a fact that makes his situation all the more complex.

What begins as a traditional, happy family of well-adjusted people slowly falls apart before his eyes. Although the reader is never quite sure why Pelzer's mother only takes her anger and **(3)** (n.) resentment_____ out on David, his **(4)** (adj.) diligent_____ attempts to survive are impressive each time he works hard to please his mother and avoid punishment. His **(5)** (n.) tactic_____(s) for survival, though desperate, are obviously necessary. Also, his mother's **(6)** (n.) denial_____ of any wrongdoing makes the reader realize how the abuse went unnoticed for such a long time and never seemed to **(7)** (v.) wane_____. This story also provides a lesson to students majoring in human services to consider the **(8)** (n.) plight_____ of children who face such emotional abandonment and **(9)** (v.) strive_____ through endurance.

Because *A Child Called "It"* is told in the voice of a young boy in the present tense, the author **(10)** (adv.) magnificently_____ depicts the events so that they seem immediate, frustrating, and, at times, frightening. The author's fear is a striking constant that prompts his audience to rapidly read on to keep Pelzer out of danger.

4 Visual Connection

Write a caption for this picture using one of the words from the box. (Answers will vary.)

inhabitants	magnificently	monument	policy

George Pngratz

_____

_____

_____

_____

_____

_____

5 Analogies

Choose the word that best completes the analogy.

1. blunt: dull :: sharp : ___a___
   a. acute   b. candid   c. diverse

2. dishonest : lying :: honest : ___c___
   a. acute   b. diverse   c. candid

3. exaggerate : overstate :: upset : ___b___
   a. intertwine   b. overwhelm   c. motivate

4. interest : apathy :: indifference : ___a___
   a. zeal   b. cathedral   c. inhabitant

5. cottage : mansion :: chapel : ___b___
   a. bank   b. cathedral   c. solstice

6. selfishness : conflict :: injustice : ___c___
   a. ambition   b. zeal   c. boycott

3

7. mean : friendly :: cruel : ___c___
   a. competitive   b. acute   c. genial

8. insincere : honest :: biased : ___a___
   a. tolerant   b. eloquent   c. ornamental

9. conversation : discuss :: goal : ___b___
   a. inequality   b. mobilize   c. cathedral

10. win : practice :: action : ___b___
    a. display   b. motivate   c. specialize

UNIT 4 Vocabulary in Math, Science and Technology

CHAPTER 11

Vocabulary and Mathematics for Business

Get Ready to Read About Mathematics for Business

When studying mathematics, college students quickly recognize the importance of knowing the vocabulary in order to work through a problem successfully. Remember the word problems you encountered from previous years of math homework? Since they involve reading, the key to solving them often lies in the vocabulary. Before you read, recall what you have learned about the following word parts.

1. The suffix *-tion* means <u>state or condition</u> and indicates a <u>noun</u>.

2. The suffix *-ate* means <u>cause to become</u> and indicates a <u>verb</u>.

| application | finance charge | interest | product | sum |
| calculate | indicator | investment | quotient | yield |

MATHEMATICS IN OUR LIVES

Mathematics is very much a part of our lives. We use mathematics when we **calculate** the amount of money we earn, the **interest** and **finance charges** on our loans, the interest earned on our **investments**, and the cost of those things most important to our future.

Many business **application** problems require mathematics. We must read the words carefully to decide how to solve the problem.

Look for **indicators** in the application problem—words that indicate the necessary operations—either addition, subtraction, multiplication, or division. Some of the words appear below.

Addition	**Subtraction**	**Multiplication** **product**	**Division**	**Equals**
plus	less		divided by	is
more	subtract	double	divided into	the same as
more than	subtracted from	triple	**quotient**	equals
added to	difference	times	goes into	equal to
increased by	less than	of	divide	**yields**
sum	fewer	twice	divided	results in
total	decreased by	twice as much	equally	are
sum of	loss of		per	
increase of	minus			
gain of	take away			
+	**−**	**×**	**÷**	**=**

Note The word "and" does not indicate addition and does not appear as an indicator word above. Notice how the "and" shows the *location of an operation sign.*

The sum of 6 *and* 2 is 6 + 2
The difference of 6 *and* 2 is 6 − 2
The product of 6 *and* 2 is 6 × 2
The quotient of 6 *and* 2 is 6 ÷ 2

—Adapted from Salzman, Miller, & Clendenen, *Mathematics for Business*, 7th ed., Addison Wesley, pp. 2–3.

VISUAL VOCABULARY

When using a credit card, it is important to be aware of the monthly ___b___ banks expect you to pay.

a. application
b. finance charge

Courtesy of Microsoft.

EXERCISE 1 Context Clues

Refer to the previous passage and use context clues from the sentences below to determine the definition of each of the following words in **bold** print. Do not consult a dictionary.

1. application (ăp′lĭ-kā′shən) n.
   In class, we learned several computer **applications** that I have been able to use in practical ways in other courses.

   ___a___ **Application** means
   a. specific use.   c. waste of time.
   b. misuse.   d. profit.

2. calculate (kăl′kyə-lāt′) v.
   Our professor advised us to **calculate** the number of hours we spend in class and then multiply by two to determine how many hours we should spend studying each week.

   ___b___ **Calculate** means
   a. to be surprised.   c. reduce.
   b. figure out.   d. study.

3. finance charge (fī′năns chärj) n.
   Before you apply for a credit card, be sure to read the fine print about any **finance charge**, which is worked out monthly and is determined by the annual percentage rate (APR).

   ___b___ **Finance charge** means
   a. a paycheck.   c. dues.
   b. a fee for credit.   d. salary.

4. **indicator** (ĭn′dĭ-kā′tər) n.
   Our math teacher told us to study the problem and first make note of the **indicators,** words that tell which process to use to determine the answer.

   __c__   **Indicator** means
       a. teacher.
       b. a solution.
       c. a word clue for solving a math problem.
       d. a process of communication.

5. **interest** (ĭn′-tĕrst′) n.
   When Anthony bought his house without a down payment, he signed a 30-year mortgage agreement to pay off some of the **interest** on the loan first before making payments on the actual amount he borrowed.

   __d__   **Interest** means
       a. time.
       b. talent.
       c. sale price.
       d. money paid for the use of an amount loaned.

6. **investment** (ĭn-vĕst′mənt) n.
   Although the stock market is not always predictable, land is usually a good **investment** if you want to make money over a long period of time.

   __a__   **Investment** means
       a. something acquired for future financial benefit.
       b. an article of clothing worn under a jacket.
       c. a checkbook.
       d. a detective's job.

7. **product** (prŏd′əkt) n.
   To determine his yearly salary, Ben multiplied the amount of his monthly paycheck by 12 months, and the **product** was his annual income.

   __b__   **Product** means
       a. a sale for profit.
       b. a quantity obtained by multiplication.
       c. an item purchased over time.
       d. the ability to make a sale.

8. quotient (kwō′shənt) n.

To determine the average rainfall each year, a meteorologist—someone who studies the weather—will add the inches each day and then divide by the number of days, and the **quotient** will be the answer.

____b____ **Quotient** means

   a. number obtained by multiplying.
   b. number obtained by dividing one quantity by another.
   c. number added.
   d. number subtracted.

9. sum (sŭm) n.

The new employee was offered a large salary—the **sum** of which included stock options, a company car, a vacation home, and yearly bonuses.

____d____ **Sum** means

   a. number obtained by multiplying.
   b. number obtained by dividing.
   c. number obtained by subtracting.
   d. number obtained by adding.

10. yield (yēld) v.

Gerald's boss is concerned about the profit that all of the employees' hard work **yields**, but he also wants to make sure the workers are happy with their work conditions.

____a____ **Yield** means

   a. produce.   c. subtract.
   b. eliminate.   d. estimate.

EXERCISE **2** Word Sorts

Synonyms

Match the word to the synonyms or definitions that follow each blank.

1. __interest_____ investment; credit; accrual; gain; percentage

2. __yield_____ equals; result in; give; produce

3. __quotient_____ the amount obtained by dividing one number by another

4. __indicator_____ word or symbol that tells what mathematical process
to use

5. __application_____ use; function; practical purpose; value

Antonyms

Select the letter of the word(s) with the opposite meaning.

__b__ **6.** calculate
    a. determine   c. compute
    b. guess   d. figure

__c__ **7.** finance charge
    a. carrying charge   c. gift
    b. tax   d. any charge for credit

__c__ **8.** product
    a. amount found by   c. quotient
       multiplying   d. duplicate
    b. sum

__d__ **9.** investment
    a. credit   c. numerous
    b. increase   d. debt

__a__ **10.** sum
    a. difference   c. total
    b. increase   d. gain

EXERCISE 3 Fill in the Blank

Use context clues to determine the word that best completes each sentence.

1. Although the state budgeted $131 million for new road construction last year, this __sum__ may not be available now unless we raise taxes to add to the state's total income.

2. At the beginning of the semester, our teacher reviewed __application(s)__, such as addition, subtraction, multiplication, and division, so we could build on a strong foundation to learn new math processes.

3. Liz's monthly investment in a certificate of deposit (CD) that provided an __interest__ rate of 4.5% helped her save for a down payment on a home.

4. A student's investment in his education through studying, asking questions, focusing on understanding, and applying good study strategies often __yield__(s) academic success.

5. After he <u>calculate</u>(d) his weekly income and expenses, Glenn was able to put 10% of his paycheck in savings each month.

6. Frida reworked her math problem and discovered she had used the wrong <u>indicator</u>, thus dividing the numbers instead of multiplying.

7. The financial advisor told the college students that in order to avoid adding to their debt after graduation, they should pay off the entire balance of their credit cards each month rather than just the monthly <u>finance charge</u>.

8. "The housing boom," reported the financial analyst, "is about to slow down because banks have run out of gimmicks to attract buyers interested in real estate as an <u>investment</u> to increase their profits and yearly incomes."

9. Psychologists use IQ, or intelligence quotient, to measure the ability to learn; however, many also believe that EQ, or emotional <u>quotient</u>, measures your emotional intelligence, which can also indicate your ability to succeed.

10. To determine your current stock market profit, multiply the number of shares of stock purchased times the current rate of the stock, and then subtract that <u>product</u> by the amount you initially spent.

EXERCISE 4 Application

Using context clues, insert the vocabulary word in the appropriate blank. A part-of-speech clue is given for each vocabulary word.

Josh and Sarah have been dating since their freshman year in college, and as they began to consider their future, they realized that with such an **(1)** (n.) <u>investment</u> of their time and their emotions, they also needed to plan for a sound financial future. First, they decided to pay off not only the monthly **(2)** (n.) <u>finance charges</u> on their credit cards, but also the entire balance and then to pay cash for expenses. They also **(3)** (v.) <u>calculate(d)</u> that each of them would need to work two jobs the following summer to save a large amount of money. Next, they invested in mutual funds with the highest rate of **(4)** (n.) <u>interest</u> they could find, and they changed to a bank that offered rewards so that their savings accounts would **(5)** (v.) <u>yield</u> more at the end of the year. Another part of their plan was to avoid unnecessary spending and always consider how long they had to work to purchase an item they felt was necessary. For example, they stopped making daily trips to the local coffee shop. Instead, that became an occasional treat. The **(6)** (n.) <u>sum</u> they saved become a monthly addition to each of their mutual funds.

During his junior year, Josh, a finance major, learned that costly mistakes can occur as a result of a simple mistake in mathematics. For instance, he read about one couple who failed to use the correct **(7)** (n.) <u>indicator</u> when determining the amount they owed on their income tax. Instead of multiplying and finding the **(8)** (n.) <u>product</u>, one man divided and determined the **(9)** (n.) <u>quotient</u>. That one **(10)** (n.) <u>application</u> cost him huge penalties and fees when the Internal Revenue Service finally discovered the error several years later.

With some careful planning and a vision for their future, Josh and Sarah graduated free of debt. When they were counseled by their minister that the number one disagreement that most couples face and often divorce over is a lack of money, they realized the financial discipline they began in their junior year would also help them when they were married.

Stop and Think

 Select three words from this chapter and complete the chart. (Answers will vary.)

Word	Definition	Picture

 Visit the following site for formulas to help you in your math class; then create study cards similar to the ones in the KIM activity (see Study Tips) you just completed to help you prepare for subsequent tests.

Algebra I and Geometry Formulas **http://www.tncc.edu/faculty/ecabinet/ MTH03DocumentsTussy/Formulas03.pdf**

12 Vocabulary and Biology

Get Ready to Read About Biology

Simply stated, biology is the study of life. In fact, the root *bio* means *life* and the suffix *-ology* means the *study* or *science of*. As you read this passage, connect to facts you know about dinosaurs and discover what scientists believe may have been responsible for their extinction. Before you read, recall what you know about the following word parts.

1. The prefix *dia-* means *through*.

2. The prefix *dis-* means *separated from* or *not*.

3. The prefix *ex-* means *from, out,* or *beyond*.

4. The root *meter* means <u>measure</u>.

5. The root *syn* means *same*.

6. The root *photo* means <u>light</u>.

7. The suffix *-ic* means *like, resembling, of* and indicates an <u>adjective</u>.

8. The suffix *-tion* means *action* or *state* and indicates a <u>noun</u>.

catastrophic	diameter	extinction	mass	photosynthesis
devastation	disruption	impact	meteorite	species

CASE STUDY: DID THE DINOSAURS
DIE FROM LACK OF SUNLIGHT?

About 65 million years ago, life on Earth suffered a **catastrophic** blow. Within a short period, most of the species on the planet were destroyed. This devastating **mass extinction** eliminated more than 70% of the **species** then existing, including the dinosaurs. Triceratops, Tyrannosaurus, and all the other dinosaur species disappeared forever. Land and sea were nearly emptied of life, and it would be many millions of years before new species arose to take the places of those that had disappeared.

Most scientists believe that the **devastation** began when a gigantic **meteorite,** six miles in **diameter,** entered the atmosphere and crashed into Earth. As the meteorite plowed into the ocean at the tip of the Yucatan Peninsula, it dug a crater a mile deep and 120 miles wide. Any organism in the immediate area was, of course, immediately killed by the blast wave from the **impact.** This kind of direct destruction, however, must have been limited to a relatively small area. How then, did the meteorite impact eliminate thousands of species in all corners of the globe? In all likelihood, the most serious damage was done not by the meteorite itself, but by the lingering aftereffects of its sudden arrival. In particular, the meteorite's most damaging effect was its **disruption** of the most important chemical reaction on Earth: **photosynthesis.**

—From Audesirk, Audesirk, & Byers, *Life on Earth*,
3rd ed., p. 81.

VISUAL VOCABULARY

This view from the Hubble telescope shows the violent

and ___b___ result of a massive supernova exploding in space.

a. diameter
b. catastrophic

hubblesite.org

EXERCISE 1 Context Clues

Refer to the previous passage and use context clues from the sentences below to determine the definition of each of the following words in **bold** print. Do not consult a dictionary.

1. catastrophic (kăt′ə-strŏf′ĭk) adj.
   Because of the loss of lives and property, the recent hurricane has been called one of the most **catastrophic** natural disasters in our country's history.

   _b_ **Catastrophic** means
   - a. calming.
   - b. disastrous.
   - c. fortunate.
   - d. sensible.

2. devastation (dĕv′ə-stā′shən) n.
   After the **devastation** caused by the earthquake, many improvements resulted, including new building codes for stronger structures that can withstand the stress of similar future disasters.

   _a_ **Devastation** means
   - a. damage.
   - b. preservation.
   - c. prediction.
   - d. litter.

3. diameter (dī-ăm′ĭ-tər) n.
   An NBA basketball has a **diameter** of about 7 inches and a circumference of almost 30 inches.

   _d_ **Diameter** means
   - a. weight.
   - b. size.
   - c. distance around.
   - d. width.

4. disruption (dĭs-rŭp′shən) n.
   The fire drill during the test caused such a **disruption** in our timing and thinking that our professor allowed everyone to retest on a different day.

   _c_ **Disruption** means
   - a. order.
   - b. calm.
   - c. disturbance.
   - d. attraction.

5. extinction (ĭk-stĭngk′shən) n.
   When the American bald eagle faced possible **extinction** because of its exposure to the pesticide DDT, it was placed on the endangered list, and now eagles are more plentiful.

   _a_ **Extinction** means
   - a. death of an entire group.
   - b. survival.
   - c. improving health.
   - d. construction.

6. impact (ĭm′păkt′) n.

The **impact** of higher gas prices will be felt this winter when the cost of heating increases by 25 to 50 percent.

_____a_____ **Impact** means

a. effect.   c. bond.

b. connection.   d. difficult choice.

7. mass (măs) adj.

When a skunk wandered into our biology lab, there was a sudden **mass** exit as everyone left the room until someone from animal control arrived.

_____c_____ **Mass** means

a. pertaining to a small amount.

b. relating to a wealth.

c. on a large-scale.

d. having to do with light weight.

8. meteorite (mē′tē-ə-rīt′) n.

As it broke away from a meteoroid, the **meteorite** plunged into a nearby field, drawing the attention of people from miles away.

_____b_____ **Meteorite** means

a. planet in another galaxy.

b. portion of a meteoroid in the earth's atmosphere.

c. a star-like planet.

d. mysterious crop circles.

9. photosynthesis (fō′tō-sĭn′thĭ-sĭs) n.

Photosynthesis provides energy for almost all living things, including algae and some bacteria.

_____c_____ **Photosynthesis** means

a. chain reaction.

b. food.

c. process plants use to create energy.

d. fear of light.

10. species (spē′shēz) n.

One **species** of edible plant that is being used by the medical community is the American ginseng.

_____b_____ **Species** means

a. differences.

b. particular type of organism.

c. unusual form of mineral.

d. twins that share a few similarities.

EXERCISE **2** Word Sorts

Synonyms

Match the word to the synonyms or definitions that follow each blank.

1. <u>meteorite</u> a portion of a meteoroid; a mass of stone or metal that has fallen to earth

2. <u>photosynthesis</u> process plants use to create energy from light, water, and carbon dioxide

3. <u>catastrophic</u> harmful; tragic; woeful; calamitous

4. <u>extinction</u> death; finish; fatality; end

5. <u>diameter</u> breadth; broadness; latitude; across measure

Antonyms

Select the letter of the word(s) with the opposite meaning.

<u>d</u> **6.** mass
   a. total   c. finish
   b. complete   d. partial

<u>a</u> **7.** species
   a. one-of-a-kind   c. type
   b. kind   d. form

<u>a</u> **8.** devastation
   a. construction   c. loss
   b. destruction   d. original

<u>c</u> **9.** disruption
   a. breakdown   c. order
   b. miscommunication   d. confusion

<u>d</u> **10.** impact
   a. crash   c. shock
   b. force   d. cause

EXERCISE **3** Fill in the Blank

Use context clues to determine the word that best completes each sentence.

1. Some areas of the world such as Hawaii, the Philippines, and New Zealand are currently facing a loss of many <u>species</u> of birds.

2. <u>Meteorite(s)</u>, which can be categorized as "rock" or "metal," vary in size, and some are not discovered until many years after they have fallen to the earth.

3. After a vehicle's air bags are inflated on <u>impact</u>, the car will then have to be towed, because it will no longer be safe to drive.

4. Some of the most <u>catastrophic</u> natural disasters in our country include the Chicago Fire, the 1900 hurricane that hit Galveston, Texas, the San Francisco Earthquake, and Hurricane Katrina.

5. Some scientists believe that over half of the world's animals and plants will face <u>extinction</u> over the next 100 years if we do not do something to protect them from elimination.

6. The <u>disruption</u> of our power last night was the result of a lightning strike on a transformer in our neighborhood.

7. As plants use carbon dioxide, water, and light for <u>photosynthesis</u>, they also give off oxygen, which creates a cleaner environment; consequently, all offices with computers should house at least one green plant as an air purifier.

8. Because of their <u>mass</u> appeal, the Harry Potter books have been bestsellers all over the world.

9. On December 26, 2004, an earthquake and tsunami caused extensive <u>devastation</u> to Sri Lanka.

10. Interesting facts about the sun include its age, which is about 4.5 billion years old, and its <u>diameter</u>, which is 870,000 miles.

EXERCISE 4 Application

Using context clues, insert the vocabulary word in the appropriate blank. A part-of-speech clue is given for each vocabulary word.

Zach stared at the night sky. Tonight, the Perseid Meteor shower would take place, and he could witness as many as 60–100 meteors a minute. It was an astonishing time for him, just as it was years ago when he had witnessed a **(1)** (n.) <u>meteorite</u> plunge to the earth, lighting the sky before it landed on the side of a distant hill, leaving a crater that was 25 feet in

(2) (n.) _diameter_____. The event that night had been good luck because the next day, he pitched a perfect game in the baseball tournament. He smiled, remembering the **(3)** (adj.) _mass_____ exit of cheering fans as they jumped from the stands after watching him catch the last out. He was overwhelmed with joy that magical night.

This night, however, did not feel so magical. This time, Zach was preparing for a job interview, and he could not sleep. Instead, he was imagining the emotional **(4)** (n.) _devastation_____ he would feel if he were not offered the job. He had studied for so many years, going to school and working part-time to become a high school teacher. He had studied with a professor who was an expert in artificial **(5)** (n.) _photosynthesis_____, a process that uses light energy to change water into hydrogen gas. He had also studied with a professor who tracked several **(6)** (n.) _species_____ of Australian butterflies that were facing possible **(7)** (n.) _extinction_____. Their final exit, scientists hoped, could someday be prevented.

Because teaching had been a lifelong dream, Zach believed it would be **(8)** (adj.) _catastrophic_____ if things did not work out. He had worked twice as long as most students to earn his degree, but his father's sudden death during his sophomore year had caused a **(9)** (n.) _disruption_____ in the rhythm of his studies as well as his finances. After taking off a few semesters, however, Zach was back on track and making the dean's list, something that would have made his father proud.

One of the last things his father said to him was, "Son, always aspire to be the best version of yourself you can be. Never give up on that."

As Zach thought about those words and the **(10)** (n.) _impact_____ his father had made on his life during so many difficult times, he saw another brilliant flash of light in the distant sky just like the one he had seen as a boy.

This time he smiled. It would be a magical night after all. And tomorrow would be another victorious day.

Stop and Think

 Go to **www.dictionary.com** and explore the differences in the words below. In the space, write the definition of each.

1. Asteroid: Celestial body that revolves around the sun. Also called minor planet, planetoid.

2. Meteor: Bright trail that appears in the sky when a meteoroid is heated as it hits the earth's atmosphere.

3. Meteoroid: Solid body moving in space, that is smaller than an asteroid and at least as large as a speck of dust.

4. Meteorite: A stony or metallic mass of matter that has fallen to the earth's surface from outer space.

 Go to the following site:
http://www.emc.maricopa.edu/faculty/farabee/BIOBK/BioBookPS.html
to locate a picture of the photosynthesis process and create a drawing below.

13. Vocabulary and Marine Science

Get Ready to Read About Marine Science

Marine science is a specialized branch of biology that investigates living organisms in the water. Before you read about the manatee, consider what you know about the following words and word parts.

1. The word *extinct* means <u>no longer existing</u>.

2. The word *species* means <u>a variety or type</u>.

3. The suffix *-ish* means *like* or *resembling* and indicates an <u>adjective</u>.

4. The suffix *-tion* means *state* or *condition* and indicates a <u>noun</u>.

brackish	habitat	notch	range	snag
fluke	media	pose	refuge	tributary

MANATEES FACE ROUGH
WATERS AROUND THE GLOBE

Manatees getting hit by boats in Florida may be grabbing most of the **media** attention, but the Sunshine State is not the only place in the world where sea cows face threats.

In countries around the world, many dangers claim the lives of these gentle marine animals. They are hunted, **snagged** in fishing nets and faced with a loss of **habitat**. And in some countries, such as Jamaica, scientists say manatees could soon become extinct.

Experts believe that the basic problem is human overpopulation. Daryl Domning, a professor who spent several years in Brazil studying manatees, says, "There are just too many people everywhere."

Three species of manatees live in the world. One kind is the West Indian manatee, which includes the Florida and the Antillean manatee. A second group is the West African manatee, and the third is the Amazonian manatee.

Most countries in which manatees live have passed laws to protect the animals. These laws make killing and hunting sea cows illegal. But laws don't always help. Even in Jamaica, where there may be fewer than 100 manatees left, sea cows are dying out even though they have been protected since 1971.

In some countries, manatee meat is sold for food. Sometimes, even local wildlife officials eat sea cow meat. In parts of West Africa, for example, manatees are served as a main dish during special celebrations.

Boating also **poses** a major danger for manatees. As boat traffic increases all over the world, experts hope Florida will serve as an example. Just like Florida, the country of Belize created **refuges** for the manatees and speed zones for boats. Belize is one of the last harbors for the Antillean manatees that live in Central and South America.

West African Manatee

Similar in size and appearance to the West Indian manatee, they **range** from 10 to 12 feet long. Little is known about the species.

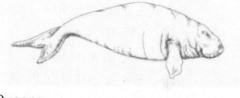

Dugong

Related to manatees, but belongs to a different family of animals. They range in size from 8 to 10 feet, with smooth skin and **notched** tail **fluke**. Lives in the Indo-Pacific.

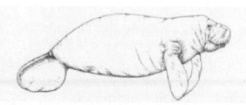

West Indian Manatee

There are two subspecies: The Florida manatee and the Antillean manatee. Both are found in salt, fresh, or **brackish** water. They range in size from 10 to 13 feet long and feed on vegetation.

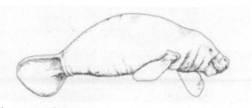

Amazon Manatee

Found in fresh waters of the Amazon River and its **tributaries**. Smallest of all manatees, with longest recorded at 9.2 feet. It has no nails on it flippers and feeds on freshwater vegetation.

–Lerman, "Manatees Face Rough Waters Around the Globe," *Daytona News-Journal*, 1 Oct. 2002, p. C1+ Reprinted with permission.

VISUAL VOCABULARY

This lake houses fish that

___b___ from perch to bass to blue gills.

   a. notch
   b. range

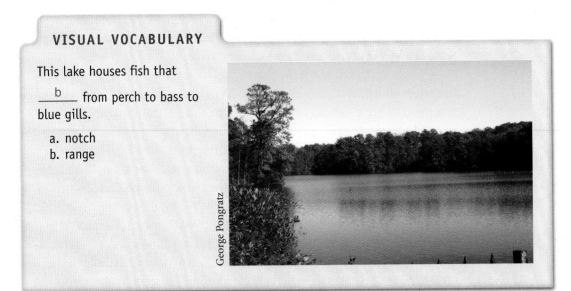

George Pongratz

EXERCISE 1 Context Clues

Refer to the previous passage and use context clues from the sentences below to determine the definition of each of the following words in **bold** print. Do not consult a dictionary.

1. brackish (brăk´ĭsh) adj.
Some government organizations are experimenting with desalinization processes on **brackish** water to remove the saltiness and make it drinkable.

___b___ **Brackish** means
   a. oily.
   b. slightly salty.
   c. polluted water.
   d. fresh water.

2. fluke (flook) n.
The **fluke** of the whale was all we could see after it took in fresh air and then dove underwater in search of more food.

___a___ **Fluke** means
   a. either of the two flattened divisions of a tail.
   b. either of the two eyes of a fish.
   c. a newborn whale.
   d. a whale blowhole.

3. habitat (hăb′ĭ-tăt′) n.

Lions, zebras, and elephants live in grassland **habitats** in Africa known as savannas.

_____a_____ **Habitat** means

    a. an area where an animal lives.
    b. areas found only in Africa.
    c. houses built for animals in the wild.
    d. zoo houses.

4. media (mē′dē-ə) n.

According to recent stories in the **media**, the medical community is beginning to recognize the benefits of video games in helping patients deal with attention deficit disorder and pain management.

_____c_____ **Media** means

    a. a means of telling fortunes.
    b. doctors.
    c. a means of mass communication.
    d. patients.

5. notch (nŏch) v.

To keep track of his long days at summer camp, Jacory **notched** each day on a walking stick he had decorated with turkey feathers.

_____d_____ **Notch** means

    a. celebrate.
    b. shape from clay.
    c. pound with great force.
    d. cut with a v-shape pattern.

6. pose (pōz) v.

George was **posed** with a problem: Should he remain loyal to the failing company and try to save it, or should he send out résumés and begin interviewing for a new job?

_____b_____ **Pose** means

    a. paint a picture.
    b. present.
    c. do as one pleases.
    d. please other people.

7. range (rānj) v.

At the time of his death in 2004, actor Marlon Brando had eleven children who **ranged** in age from 10 to 46.

_____c_____ **Range** means

    a. eliminate.
    b. notice.
    c. vary.
    d. suggest.

8. refuge (rĕf′yo͞oj) n.

Some people escape to the mountains or the seashore for a **refuge,** while others curl up in an amchair with a good book.

____c____ **Refuge** means

    a. imaginary place.
    b. ocean.

    c. safe place.
    d. mountain trail.

9. snag (snăg) v.

The young woman had two goals her senior year: earn her college degree and **snag** a rich man she could marry right after graduation.

____b____ **Snag** means

    a. complete with pride.
    b. catch unexpectedly.

    c. study.
    d. leave with great care.

10. tributary (trĭb′yə-tĕr′ē) n.

Deep Creek and Lake Maury are both **tributaries** that feed into the James River.

____d____ **Tributary** means

    a. oceanfront property.
    b. campsites.

    c. a large body of water.
    d. water that feeds into a larger body of water.

EXERCISE 2 Word Sorts

Synonyms

Match the word to the synonyms or definitions that follow each blank.

1. tributary _____ stream; brook; creek

2. media _____ radio; television; movies; newspapers

3. pose _____ present; propose; suggest; put forward

4. fluke _____ a flattened division on a whale's tale

5. range _____ vary; differ; run; fluctuate

Antonyms

Select the letter of the word(s) with the opposite meaning.

____a____ **6.** refuge

    a. exposure
    b. safe place

    c. retreat
    d. hideout

___c___ **7.** snag
     a. grab   c. give
     b. take possession   d. surround

___c___ **8.** notch
     a. indent   c. smooth
     b. carve   d. score

___d___ **9.** habitat
     a. environment   c. residence
     b. home   d. unnatural surroundings

___c___ **10.** brackish
     a. slightly salty   c. tasteless
     b. briny   d. sour

EXERCISE **3** Fill in the Blank

Use context clues to determine the word that best completes each sentence.

1. When the House Majority Leader was charged with a felony, the news
____media____ immediately jumped at the chance to cover the story
and analyze the consequences.

2. The bold, young journalist __pose(d)__ a question to the newly
elected governor, who quickly praised him for his courage.

3. On a recent whale-watching trip, we had to use binoculars to scope out
the mammals, but all we could see were the __fluke(s)__ of their
tails as they dove beneath the water.

4. Whereas perch are often found in __brackish__ waters, you would
need to go deep sea fishing to catch a marlin.

5. To overcome anxiety, some people use positive imaging, which may
involve creating a mental picture of a __refuge__ such as a safe,
quiet area in the woods or a sunny, smooth rock near a waterfall.

6. In the nearby Living Museum, we saw some American bald eagles who
remained in their natural __habitat__ within a large fence because
they had been injured previously or abused elsewhere and were no longer
able to fly.

7. The grades on the last test <u>range(d)</u> from 88 to 100 percent, and our professor was so pleased she played "We Are the Champions" while she returned the papers.

8. Years ago, our college baseball team started a tradition in which a player who hit a grand slam was allowed to <u>notch</u> a special Louisville Slugger bat and then sign his name and the date next to the v-shaped cut.

9. After going to the career center and learning about posting online résumés, he was able to <u>snag</u> a new job with a company on the West Coast.

10. In an effort to diminish some water pollution, several organizations are working to reduce the amount of nitrogen and phosphorous in each <u>tributary</u> that feeds into the Chesapeake Bay.

EXERCISE 4 Application

Using context clues, insert the vocabulary word in the appropriate blank. A part-of-speech clue is given for each vocabulary word.

Tyra sloshed through the wetlands, collecting samples of the **(1)** (adj.) <u>brackish</u> water to test for salt levels later in the lab. As she moved through an area, she **(2)** (v.) <u>notched</u> a tree limb so she would not repeat the testing procedure unnecessarily. The water in this stream was a **(3)** (n.) <u>tributary</u> that eventually led to the Mississippi River, so it was also important to test for pollutants in order to ensure the water was safe. The project had recently attracted the attention of the **(4)** (n.) <u>media</u>, and Tyra hoped her interview with the television crew would be viewed favorably. If she did her job well, and if the interview was convincing, then these wetlands would continue to serve as a **(5)** (n.) <u>habitat</u> for the plants and animals that so readily thrived here. In addition, she could convince government officials that using pesticides to kill mosquitoes would not be necessary if they created a

(6) (n.) <u>refuge</u> for dragonflies and bats, both of which eat mosquitoes.

Tyra remembered when a journalist recently **(7)** (v.) <u>posed</u> the question, "Why should we protect this area when we could develop it and create a larger tax base for the state?" She shivered at the thought. Often developers were allowed to build on property the Army Corps of Engineers had declared protected. The reasons, though, usually **(8)** (v.) <u>range</u> (d) from the need for more affordable housing to creating ways to avoid flooding in the event of future hurricanes.

Her desire to protect the environment began when she was in the third grade and read a story about fishermen who would harpoon whales or hook and mangle one of their **(9)** (n.) <u>flukes</u>. From then on, she explored nature whenever she had a chance. Protecting the environment became her passion, and when she was able to **(10)** (v.) <u>snag</u> this internship during college, she recognized that such opportunities do not happen twice. Again, this was her chance to make a difference and help protect the world for the next generation.

Stop and Think

Using three vocabulary words from this chapter, summarize the passage about manatees in 3-2-1 summary below. (Answers may vary.)

3-Write three signs that manatees are in danger: <u>They are hunted. They are snagged in nets. They face a loss of habitat.</u>

2-List two reasons manatees are in danger: <u>Overpopulation has caused problems. They are sometimes hunted for food. Boaters pose problems.</u>

1-Tell one thing people can do to protect them: <u>Speed zones for boats can be established. We can create refuges for the manatees.</u>

Go to **www.etymonline.com** and research the word *tributary* to see how it evolved from the word *tribute*. Write the etymology (word history) in the space below.

From the Latin word *tributarius* that means "liable to tax," the word *tributary* first

appeared in 1382 to mean "paying tribute." In 1432, it took on a noun form to mean

"one who pays tribute." In 1822, the word *tributary* was used to mean a "Stream that

flows into a larger body." To connect stream and taxes, think of both moving into

larger areas of collection.

14 Vocabulary and Computer Technology

Get Ready to Read About Computer Technology

Many college students are pursuing a degree in computer science, which is considered a hot field. Some plan to be programmers, some systems analysts, some web page designers, and some computer technicians. Before you read the passage about e-commerce, consider what you know about the following word parts.

1. The prefix *inter-* means between   .

2. The root *leg* means *law*.

3. The root *nym* means name   .

4. The suffix *-al* means *like* or *related to* and indicates an adjective   .

5. The suffix *-ent* means *like* or *related to* and indicates an adjective   .

6. The suffix *-ity* means *quality* or *trait* and indicates a noun   .

7. The suffix *-ive* means *like* or *related to* and indicates an adjective   .

anonymity	fraudulent	intercept	lucrative	security
cloak	global	legitimate	potential	subject

THE E-COMMERCE SECURITY ENVIRONMENT

For most law-abiding citizens, the Internet holds the promise of a **global** marketplace, providing access to people and businesses worldwide. For criminals, the Internet created entirely new—and **lucrative**—ways to steal. From products and service to cash to information, it's all there for the taking on the Internet.

It's also less risky to steal online. The **potential** for **anonymity** on the Internet **cloaks** many criminals in **legitimate**-looking identities, allowing them to place **fraudulent** orders with online merchants, steal information by **intercepting** e-mail, or simply shut down e-commerce sites by using software viruses. In the end, however, the actions of such cybercriminals are costly for both businesses and consumers, who are then **subjected** to higher prices and additional **security**.

—From Laudon & Traver, *E-Commerce*, 2nd ed., p. 252.
Copyright by Pearson Education.

VISUAL VOCABULARY

Because computers have opened a new world and expanded our ways to communicate with people from other areas outside our community, they have provided

a more ___a___ connection.

a. global
b. lucrative

Susan Pongratz

EXERCISE **1** Context Clues

Refer to the previous passage and use context clues from the sentences below to determine the definition of each of the following words in **bold** print. Do not consult a dictionary.

1. anonymity (ăn′ə-nĭ m-tē) n.
On a condition of **anonymity**, the witness agreed to testify if the FBI could keep his identity a secret.

_____c_____ **Anonymity** means
    a. state of being identified.   c. state of being unknown.
    b. same meaning.   d. having an opposite meaning.

2. cloak (klōk) v.
The boys were **cloaked** by the cover of darkness as they peered through the tree branches and watched the pirates study the treasure map by the camp fire.

_____a_____ **Cloak** means
    a. disguise.   c. display.
    b. uncover.   d. dream.

3. fraudulent (frô′jə-lənt) adj.
The FBI is responsible for investigating **fraudulent** activities that include white-collar crimes such as the filing of false insurance claims.

_____a_____ **Fraudulent** means
    a. characterized by dishonesty.   c. predictable.
    b. fair.   d. characterized by honesty.

4. global (glō′bəl) adj.
In order to prevent a major epidemic of Avian flu, there must be a **global** response of the medical community around the world to educate and protect the public.

_____b_____ **Global** means
    a. local.   c. national.
    b. worldwide.   d. small area.

5. intercept (ĭn′tər-sĕpt′) v.
The college football team has earned its #3 position through excellent passing and rushing, but the safety's ability to **intercept** the ball and run for a touchdown at least once each game may make this team unstoppable by the end of the season.

___d___ **Intercept** means
- a. distribute.
- b. plead.
- c. determine the meaning of something.
- d. catch.

6. legitimate (lə-jĭt′ə-mĭt) adj.
Money-laundering schemes involve **legitimate** businesses such as real estate firms or restaurants that can take in and transfer large amounts of cash from illegal enterprises and make them seem lawful.

___b___ **Legitimate** means
- a. illegal.
- b. lawful.
- c. unsuitable.
- d. inappropriate.

7. lucrative (lōō′krə-tĭv) adj.
To finance their tuition, Joe and Tom began a **lucrative** business building and renting loft beds to college students, and eventually they made enough money to pay for graduate school as well.

___c___ **Lucrative** means
- a. poor.
- b. failing.
- c. profitable.
- d. genuine.

8. potential (pə-tĕn′shəl) n.
Although the disagreement had the **potential** to develop into a major fight, the cool-headed supervisor stepped in and was able to encourage the parties to calm down and discuss the problem.

___b___ **Potential** means
- a. impossibility.
- b. ability.
- c. surprise.
- d. help.

9. security (sĭ-kyŏŏr′ĭ-tē) n.
If you need assistance walking to your car late in the evening, please call campus police for the **security** of having someone escort you safely across campus.

___d___ **Security** means
- a. danger.
- b. continuation.
- c. entertainment.
- d. protection.

10. subject (səb-jĕkt′) v.

Until he was finally diagnosed with Lyme disease, my roommate was **subjected** to a variety of medical tests.

___a___ **Subject** means

a. cause to experience.   c. strike unnecessarily.
b. disregard.   d. smooth quietly.

EXERCISE **2** Word Sorts

Synonyms

Match the word to the synonyms or definitions that follow each blank.

1. _security_ _____ safety; assurance; safeguard; defense

2. _intercept_ _____ catch; break in; ambush; cut in

3. _cloak_ _____ conceal; hide; camouflage; cover

4. _subject_ _____ expose; experience; endure; tolerate

5. _potential_ _____ power; capability; aptitude; power

Antonyms

Select the letter of the word(s) with the opposite meaning.

___a___ **6.** anonymity
    a. well known   c. insecure
    b. unidentified   d. unknown

___a___ **7.** lucrative
    a. unprofitable   c. popular
    b. successful   d. unimaginative

___b___ **8.** fraudulent
    a. deceitful   c. criminal
    b. honest   d. swindling

___b___ **9.** global
    a. international   c. universal
    b. restricted   d. all-inclusive

___d___ **10.** legitimate
    a. legal   c. understood
    b. customary   d. unlawful

EXERCISE ▋3▋ Fill in the Blank

Use context clues to determine the word that best completes each sentence.

1. During the Cold War, U.S. planes used to <u>intercept</u> Soviet air bombers off the coast of Virginia while they were en route to Cuba.

2. Visiting football teams at the University of Iowa's Kennick Stadium are <u>subject(ed)</u> to a pink locker room because the former head coach, a psychology major, believed the passive color would have a calming effect on the opponents.

3. Although the house needs some major repairs, it has the <u>potential</u> to become a showplace someday.

4. After her divorce was final, Ella no longer needed <u>anonymity</u> to write about her experiences living with an abusive spouse, so she allowed her real name to be used in the byline of her article.

5. The World Health Organization has announced that the <u>global</u> effect of the bird flu virus could include the deaths of 7.4 million people worldwide.

6. To ensure that a contractor is operating a <u>legitimate</u> business, insist that he produce credentials as proof that he is licensed and bonded.

7. Through imagination, good timing, and hard work, Fred Smith turned a college project into the <u>lucrative</u> business we now know as Federal Express.

8. Long-term municipal bonds offer more financial <u>security</u> than stock investments in which you must risk your money to make more money.

9. Many get-rich quick schemes, such as the Ponzi Pyramid, have turned out to be <u>fraudulent</u> enterprises that only benefit those at the top of the scale.

10. <u>Cloak(ed)</u> in camouflage fatigues, the soldiers snaked their way through the jungle, hoping to avoid detection by the enemy.

EXERCISE **4** Application

Using context clues, insert the vocabulary word in the appropriate blank. A part-of-speech clue is given for each vocabulary word.

The "Hang-and-Run" artist—known only as "Banksy" to protect his **(1)** (adj.) <u>anonymity</u>—has earned fame for his ability to slip in and out of famous museums, despite the cameras installed for reasons of **(2)** (n.) <u>security</u> and hang up his own artwork. He **(3)** (v.) <u>cloaks</u> himself in disguises that include long beards, glasses, and hats, and installs his own framed paintings among the work by great artists such as Renoir, Monet or Cezanne. So far, he has only been caught by surveillance cameras after the deed, but no one has been able to **(4)** (v.) <u>intercept</u> him during the actual crime.

Banksy's scheme is not a **(5)** (adj.) <u>legitimate</u> way to have artwork on display in a major museum. In fact, it is considered a crime. Not only is it illegal, but also each hang-and-run occurrence **(6)** (v.) <u>subjects</u> the museum administrators to embarrassing publicity. Nor is this a **(7)** (adj.) <u>lucrative</u> opportunity, since Banksy does not gain financially from his crime. Instead, it would seem he enjoys the personal satisfaction of displaying his artwork and tricking museum authorities. The artwork itself is also often **(8)** (adj.) <u>fraudulent</u>. For example, his painting *You Have Beautiful Eyes* is an oil painting he found and to which he added a gas mask. Still, Banksy calls himself a painter and a decorator.

How does he sneak in and out? He reported reading biographies about the famous escape artist, Harry Houdini, to learn tips on how to elude detection. In addition, Banksy explained that in a museum, most people do not pay attention to others so he usually finds the location offers him the **(9)** (adj.) <u>potential</u> of being invisible to visitors.

When asked why he bothered to commit the crime, Banksy said that he didn't want to get stuck in the same line of work all his life. This current line of work has earned him some **(10)** (adj.) global _____ attention, beginning first in Europe and now moving to the United States.

Source: *http://www.npr.org/templates/story/story.php?*
storyId=4559961 March 24, 2005, *All Things Considered*,
interviewed By Michel Norris/ Retrieved 8/25/05

Stop and Think

Go to **http://www.npr.org/templates/story/story.php?storyId=4559961** to view one of Banksy's paintings. Use at least one vocabulary word and write your opinion of the scheme.

_____

_____

_____

Go to **www.dictionary.com** to explore the other parts of speech for the following words:

Noun	Adjective	Verb
1. cloak		1. cloak
2. interception		2. intercept
3. security	3. secure	3. secure
4. fraud	4. fraudulent	

4

Review Test
Chapters 11-14

1 Word Parts

Match the definitions in Column 2 to the word parts in Column 1.

Column 1		Column 2	
c	**1.** photo	a.	separated from; not
f	**2.** syn-	b.	law
h	**3.** dia-	c.	light
i	**4.** nym	d.	between
d	**5.** inter-	e.	for; forward
b	**6.** leg	f.	together; with
j	**7.** -ive	g.	one who; one that
a	**8.** dis-	h.	through
g	**9.** -ent	i.	name
e	**10.** pro-	j.	of; like; related to; being

2 Fill in the Blank

Use context clues to determine the best word from the box to complete each sentence.

anonymity	diameter	intercept	mass	quotient
calculate	finance charges	legitimate	notch	snag

1. After considering the amount of <u>finance charges</u> that would be attached to the credit card balance, we decided not to complete the application; instead, we shopped around for a better rate.

163

4

2. In our division problem, we realized we had the wrong dividend, which resulted in the incorrect quotient_____.

3. Because of his popularity, author Mark Twain traveled throughout Europe and at each stop spoke to masses_____ of people who gathered in large groups to experience his quick wit firsthand.

4. Most residential water pipes are five-eighths of an inch in diameter_____, while commercial pipes are three-fourths of an inch.

5. The F15 pilot knew his job was to intercept_____ the unidentified aircraft.

6. Jamaahl looked over the exam and calculate_____(d) how long each essay question would take.

7. Before cutting the Fraser fir, Ben cut a notch_____ in the trunk.

8. The cat will snag_____ the furniture with her claws if she does not have a scratching post to use.

9. When you register through your college e-mail address at **www.facebook.com**, you can look at the photographs of the friends of people you know without revealing yourself, under the cloak of anonymity_____.

10. On the first day of class, our professor announced, "You must be present to win; therefore, no absences are allowed, even those with legitimate_____ excuses."

3 Book Connection

Use context clues to determine the best word from the box to complete each sentence.

brackish	habitat	potential	meteorite	security
cloaked	lucrative	product	refuge	species

BOY'S LIFE

Author Robert McCammon is best known as a science fiction writer, and his 1991 novel *Boy's Life* has all of the elements of a great story. The novel

4

is narrated by Cory Mackenson, who recalls his life in the small town of Zephyr, Alabama, in 1962 when he was twelve. Rich with many details, the story yields unpredictable twists in the plot, which is filled with fantasy, love, and the perennial theme of good versus evil. It is also an adventure complete with a monster, an unknown **(1)** species submerged in its **(2)** habitat in the **(3)** brackish waters of a nearby lake, as well as a blazing **(4)** meteorite that trails from space and lands in the hills beyond the town. Still, **(5)** security in the town was not an issue.

Although the story takes place during the turbulent sixties, Zephyr is the **(6)** refuge that provides a place of safety for many, including an evil murderer who remains **(7)** cloaked in mystery until the narrator uncovers the truth. And, like most small towns, there are also some oddities such as the young man with a **(8)** lucrative inheritance and social prominence, who, because of his wealth and power, is allowed to conduct business in town wearing nothing but a smile.

This is a tale of growing up as seen through the eyes of a young man all too aware of his own imperfections. For example, while he loves words and creating stories, he fails miserably at math problems, rarely able to determine the **(9)** product of a multiplication equation. Instead, he has the **(10)** potential to be a great storyteller. This is also a story of his family's love and the devotion his parents have for each other as well as their son; the dreams his parents must put aside are a testimony to their lifetime of commitment. Finally, the book reminds us of the bonds of friendship—that closeness that we cherish as children and how much we value those connections throughout our lives.

4 Visual Connection

Write a caption for this picture using one of the words from the box. (Answers will vary.)

| devastation | extinction | impact | sum | interest | indicator | media |

George Pongratz

_____

_____

_____

_____

_____

_____

_____

_____

_____

5 Analogies

Choose the word that best completes the analogy.

1. hotel : reservation :: math problem : __b__
   a. investment   b. application   c. councilor

2. course : diploma :: money : __c__
   a. application   b. tributary   c. investment

3. human : cooking :: plant : __a__
   a. photosynthesis   b. disruption   c. extinction

4. peace : noise :: order : __c__
   a. tributary   b. fluke   c. disruption

5. round : circular :: vary : __a__
   a. range   b. subject   c. yield

4

6. content : dissatisfied :: joyous : ___b___
   a. happy   b. catastrophic   c. fun

7. city : street :: ocean : ___b___
   a. fluke   b. tributary   c. quotient

8. road : fork :: tail : ___a___
   a. fluke   b. finance charge   c. sum

9. light : dark :: honest : ___b___
   a. global   b. fraudulent   c. legitimate

10. small : large :: local : ___a___
   a. global   b. diameter   c. quotient

UNIT 5 Vocabulary in Communications and Humanities

CHAPTER 15. Vocabulary and Interpersonal Communication

Get Ready to Read About Interpersonal Communication

Interpersonal communication involves how we relate to ourselves and others through what we say, how we say it, and what we leave unsaid. It explores the power of words as well as body language. Many colleges require interpersonal communication as a core course because college is a place to learn how to communicate more effectively. Before you read this selection, recall what you know about the following word parts:

1. The prefix *con-* means <u>with, together</u>.

2. The prefix *re-* means <u>again</u>.

3. The root *fer* means *carry*.

4. The suffix *-al* means *of, like, related to, being* and indicates an <u>adjective</u>.

168

5. The suffix *-ity* means *quality, trait* and indicates a <u>noun</u>   .

6. The suffix *-ive* means *of, like, related to, being* and indicates an

<u>adjective</u>   .

---

adjust	confront	inference	literal	relational
authority	engage	inter	oration	sensitive

SURFACE AND DEPTH LISTENING

In Shakespeare's *Julius Caesar*, Marc Antony, in giving the funeral **oration** for Caesar, says, "I come to bury Caesar, not to praise him. The evil men do lives after them;/ The good is oft **interred** with their bones." And later: "For Brutus is an honourable man;/ So are they all, all honourable men." But Antony, as we know, did come to praise Caesar and to convince the crowd that Brutus was not an honorable man.

In most messages there's an obvious meaning. You arrive at this clear meaning from a **literal** reading of the words and sentences. But there's often another level of meaning. Consider some often heard messages. Carol asks you how you like her new haircut. On one level, the meaning is clear. Do you like the haircut? But there's also another, perhaps more important, level. Carol is asking you to say something positive about her appearance. The same is true for the parent who complains about working hard at the office or in the home. The parent, on a deeper level, may be asking for an expression of appreciation. The child who talks about the unfairness of the other children on the playground may be asking for comfort and love. To grasp these other meanings you need to **engage** in depth listening.

If you respond only to the surface-level message, you miss making meaningful contact with the other person's feelings and needs. If you say to the parent, "You're always complaining. I bet you really love working hard," you fail to respond to his or her real need. You have ignored his or her need for support and encouragement. To **adjust** your surface and depth listening, think about the following guidelines:

Focus on both verbal and nonverbal messages. Look for both consistent and inconsistent packages of messages. Use these as guides for drawing **inferences** about the speaker's meaning. Ask questions when in doubt. Listen also to what is omitted. Remember, speakers communicate by what they don't say as well as by what they do say.

*Listen for both content and **relational** messages.* For example, take the student who always challenges the teacher. On one level, this student may be disagreeing with the content. Yet, on another level, the student may be **confronting** the teacher's **authority.** The teacher needs to listen and respond to both types of messages.

Make special note of statements that refer back to the speaker. People usually talk about themselves. Whatever a person says is, in part, a result of who that person is. So listen carefully to those personal messages.

Don't ignore the literal meaning of a message in trying to find the hidden meaning. Balance your listening. Reply to the different levels of meaning in the messages of others, just as you would like others to respond to you. Be **sensitive.** Listen carefully, but don't be too eager to uncover hidden messages.

—Adapted from DeVito, Joseph A. *The Interpersonal
Communication Book,* 12th ed., p. 125.
Published by Allyn & Bacon, Boston, MA.
Copyright by Pearson Education.

VISUAL VOCABULARY

This man is ___b___ in a cell
phone conversation.

   a. interred
   b. engaged

Courtesy of Microsoft.

EXERCISE 1 Context Clues

Refer to the previous passage and use context clues from the sentences below to determine the definition of each of the following words in **bold** print. Do not consult a dictionary.

1. adjust (ə-jŭst′) v.
Naomi was excited about her plans to study abroad in Rome even though she would have to **adjust** to new roommates.

  ___c___ **Adjust** means
     a. confuse.   c. get used to.
     b. disrupt.   d. avoid.

2. authority (ə-thôr′ĭ-tē) n.
Whereas some college presidents enjoy the command and **authority** of their leadership position, ours willingly meets and talks with students and even teaches a freshman seminar.

____b____ **Authority** means

    a. servant.   c. disadvantage.

    b. power.   d. obstacle.

3. confront (kən-frŭnt′) v.

During football season, the entire city of Knoxville becomes a sea of orange, the school color, each time the University of Tennessee Volunteers prepare to **confront** their opponents.

____a____ **Confront** means

    a. challenge.   c. praise.

    b. ignore.   d. retreat from.

4. engage (ĕn-gāj′) v.

One of the best ways to **engage** someone in a conversation is to ask a question that requires more than a simple yes or no answer.

____a____ **Engage** means

    a. interest.   c. break off.

    b. send.   d. surrender.

5. inference (ĭn′fər-əns) n.

Crime scene investigators must consider the facts, make **inferences** about the evidence, and then find proof to support their conclusions.

____b____ **Inference** means

    a. suggestion.   c. effect.

    b. conclusion.   d. agreement.

6. inter (ĭn-tûr′) v.

Because of a shortage of space, some countries require that bodies now be **interred** on top of others because the stacking uses less land.

____c____ **Inter** means

    a. dig up.   c. bury.

    b. avoid.   d. begin.

7. literal (lĭt′ər-əl) adj.

In our Spanish class, the teacher reads aloud questions; then we have to write the **literal** English translation and follow that with our answer in Spanish.

____d____ **Literal** means

    a. inaccurate.   c. creative.

    b. imaginative.   d. word for word.

8. oration (ô-rā′shən) n.

Athough giving a perfect **oration** may not be your talent, you can learn to be a good public speaker by practicing strategies we learn in speech class.

___a___ **Oration** means

    a. speech.   c. accurate translation.

    b. decoration.   d. simple request.

9. relational (rĭ-lā′shə-nəl) adj.

When a child tries to start an argument with a parent, a wise adult will avoid a confrontation and instead look for a **relational** cause such as difficulty at school or a disagreement with friends as the real source of the frustration.

___b___ **Relational** means

    a. relative.   c. recreational.

    b. connecting.   d. serious.

10. sensitive (sĕn′sĭ-tĭv) adj.

Many new parents become so **sensitive** to the needs of their baby that they begin to recognize differences in cries that indicate hunger, boredom, fear, or loneliness.

___c___ **Sensitive** means

    a. confused.   c. tuned in.

    b. slow.   d. tired.

EXERCISE 2 Word Sorts

Synonyms

Match the word to the synonyms or definitions that follow each blank.

1. relational_____ having to do with a connection between two things

2. oration_____ speech; address; talk; monologue

3. engage_____ participate; embark on; activate; take part

4. authority_____ power; boss; brains; brass

5. inter_____ bury, lay to rest

Antonyms

Select the letter of the word(s) with the opposite meaning.

_c_ **6.** literal

    a. actual   c. figurative

    b. accurate   d. opposition

_d_ **7.** confront

    a. challenge   c. surprise

    b. face   d. ignore

_b_ **8.** inference

    a. conclusion   c. obstacle

    b. hint   d. respect

_a_ **9.** adjust

    a. upset   c. be satisfied

    b. unwind   d. consider

_a_ **10.** sensitive

    a. cruel   c. tender

    b. aware   d. touched

EXERCISE **3** Fill in the Blank

Use context clues to determine the word that best completes each sentence.

1. To children who apply _literal_____ interpretations to most situations, the comment, "You've grown a foot!" can be very confusing.

2. Although it is necessary to be _sensitive_____ to others' needs when a disaster occurs, you must also be realistic about what contribution you can make alone and try to combine your efforts with other people or groups to make a larger impact.

3. No matter how hard you practice for an athletic event, the outcome will be determined by how well you play the day of the big game when you _confront_____ the visiting team.

4. To develop skills in _oration_____, a student must learn to compose a meaningful speech and deliver it with confidence and passion, while maintaining eye contact with the audience.

5. In the event of the loss of the country's president and vice-president, the _authority_____ passes to the Speaker of the House.

6. Although the victim was quickly <u>inter</u>_____(red) after his death, the medical examiner was asked to have the body exhumed for further examination after new evidence was presented.

7. Creating a good habit requires practice and determination to <u>adjust</u>_____ to a new way of life.

8. Osteopathic medicine recognizes the connection of our mental, emotional, <u>relational</u>_____, and spiritual states to our whole health.

9. To develop our critical thinking skills, our philosophy professor gives us riddles and brain teasers that require us to make <u>inference</u>_____(s) to find accurate solutions.

10. Many business schools offer etiquette workshops to teach students ways to <u>engage</u>_____ in conversations and small talk at office functions, job interviews, and networking opportunities.

EXERCISE 4 Application

Using context clues, insert the vocabulary word in the appropriate blank. A part-of-speech clue is given for each vocabulary word.

Located at Arlington National Cemetery, the Tomb of the Unknown Soldier is the place where several soldiers are **(1)** (v.) <u>inter</u>_____(red). Following a moving **(2)** (n.) <u>oration</u>_____ by Congressman Hamilton Fish, Jr., the tomb was established on November 11, 1921. Under the **(3)** (n.) <u>authority</u>_____ of the 66th Congress, the tomb became the final resting place of an American soldier killed in France during World War I. Since then, the bodies of unidentified soldiers who were **(4)** (v.) <u>engage</u>_____(d) in combat during World War II, the Korean Conflict, and the Vietnam War have also been buried in the tomb. This tradition is consistent with the original intention to honor all of those who have fallen in time of war and to ensure that no sacrifice is forgotten. The public was quickly able to **(5)** (v.) <u>adjust</u>_____ to the idea of burying soldiers from subsequent wars. In fact, the **(6)** (adj.) <u>relational</u> connection of each body is a reminder of the similarities that exist with each war.

The Tomb of the Unknown Soldier is both a **(7)** (adj.) <u>literal</u> final resting place as well as a figurative symbol for other soldiers who are still considered missing. This has always been a **(8)** (adj.) <u>sensitive</u> issue for the military to **(9)** (v.) <u>confront</u>, because leaders hope all service people who have sacrificed their lives will be identified. When visiting Arlington National Cemetery, however, one always makes the **(10)** (n.) <u>inference</u> that it is a place of honor and reverence.

–Adapted from http://www.tombguard.org/history.html

Stop and Think

Select a word from the chapter and create a pyramid summary following the guidelines below. (Answers will vary.)

Word: _____

Definition: _____

Antonyms: _____

Synonyms: _____

Sample Sentence: _____

Go to **http://www.tombguard.org/history.html** and read the detailed history of the Tomb of the Unknown Soldier. Then select one word from this chapter that best summarizes the passage. Write the word, the definition, and your reason for selecting that word. (Answers will vary.)

_____

_____

_____

_____

CHAPTER 16

Vocabulary and Literature

Get Ready to Read About Literature

When reading literature, you will recognize there are both literal and figurative meanings. Sometimes you will have to make inferences, or conclusions, about what the author intends. This selection by William Shakespeare contains lines that are often quoted, and it is considered an example of an extended metaphor. To understand it fully, consider the definitions of the following terms, which will provide a background for your future reading of literature.

1. **Metaphor:** A comparison of two unlike things without using the words *like* or *as*. For example, Shakespeare compares people and life to actors in a play: "All the world's a stage."

2. **Simile:** A comparison of two unlike things using the words *like* or *as*. For instance, instead of saying "All the world's a stage," the speaker would say "All the world is *like* a stage."

| ballad | oath | pard | satchel | treble |
| mewl | oblivion | sans | saw | woeful |

All the world's a stage,
And all the men and women merely players:
They have their exits and their entrances;
And one man in his time plays many parts,
His acts being seven ages. At first the infant,
Mewling and puking in the nurse's arms.
And then the whining school-boy, with his **satchel**
And shining morning face, creeping like snail
Unwillingly to school. And then the lover,
Sighing like furnace, with a **woeful ballad**
Made to his mistress' eyebrow. Then a soldier,
Full of strange **oaths** and bearded like the **pard,**
Jealous in honour, sudden and quick in quarrel,
Seeking the bubble reputation
Even in the cannon's mouth. And then the justice,
In fair round belly with good capon lined,
With eyes severe and beard of formal cut,
Full of wise **saws** and modern instances;
And so he plays the part. The sixth age shifts
Into the lean and slipper'd pantaloon,
With spectacles on nose and pouch on side,
His youthful hose, well saved, a world too wide
For his shrunk shank; and his big manly voice,
Turning again toward childish **treble,** pipes
And whistles in his sound. Last scene of all,
That ends this strange eventful history,
Is second childishness and mere **oblivion,**
Sans teeth, sans eyes, sans taste, sans every thing.

—*As You Like It*, Act II, sc. vii.

VISUAL VOCABULARY

The Globe Theater of London was the site of Shakespeare's plays and the singing of some memorable ___b___.

a. pards
b. ballads

Elizabeth Pongratz

EXERCISE **1** Context Clues

Refer to the previous passage and use context clues from the sentences below to determine the definition of each of the following words in **bold** print. Do not consult a dictionary.

1. ballad (băl′əd) n.
One of the saddest **ballads** is the tragic song from Scotland about the story of Barbara Allen and her beloved Sir James of the Grave.

___b___ **Ballad** means
  a. letter.   c. cheerful greeting.
  b. song that tells a story.   d. religious hymn.

2. mewl (myōol) v.
We could not sleep last night because of the brilliant full moon, especially when the stray cats on the fence beneath our bedroom window began to **mewl** pitifully.

___a___ **Mewl** means
  a. cry or whimper.   c. chew slowly.
  b. rest quietly.   d. correct or approve.

3. oath (ōth) n.

Until my brother learned to memorize the Boy Scout **Oath,** he walked around the house practicing the pledge for days.

    _d_   **Oath** means

    a. uniform.   c. history.

    b. question.   d. promise.

4. oblivion (ə-blĭv′ē-ən) n.

"No matter how hard I study," complained Kristy, "I scare myself so that everything I have studied vanishes into **oblivion,** and my state of forgetfulness then causes me to panic."

    _d_   **Oblivion** means

    a. sudden surprise.   c. place of honor.

    b. formal arrangement.   d. condition of being forgotten.

5. pard (pärd) n.

For Halloween, Alyssa, Madison, and Morgan dressed in simple **pard** costumes by using black tights, leotards, braided tails, and painted whiskers so that they looked like characters from the Broadway musical *Cats.*

    _a_   **Pard** means

    a. leopard or any large cat.   c. favorite household pet.

    b. parrot or other exotic bird. d. witch.

6. sans (sănz) prep. (French)

My father, who does not like to wear a tie, always cringes when he receives an invitation to any formal occasion; instead, he prefers dressy casual affairs that require jacket **sans** tie.

    _b_   **Sans** means

    a. with.   c. matching.

    b. without.   d. contrasting.

7. satchel (săch′əl) n.

Late as usual, Professor Cardinal hurried down the brick path toward the lecture hall with papers flying out of his **satchel** and autumn leaves swirling around him.

    _c_   **Satchel** means

    a. lecture hall.   c. briefcase.

    b. lecture notes.   d. research.

8. saw (sô) n.

After taking a course in creative writing, my roommate began keeping a personal journal, which is a collection of her favorite poems, proverbs, quotations, old **saws**, and artwork.

___d___ **Saw** means

    a. writing tool.   c. artist canvas.

    b. sculpting tool.   d. wise saying.

9. treble (trĕb′əl) n.

When Kim sings selections from Broadway musicals, we try to politely endure her **treble**, but we always end up sneaking away before she has finished one song.

___b___ **Treble** means

    a. double vision.   c. beautiful words.

    b. shrill sound.   d. soft whispering.

10. woeful (wō′fəl) adj.

Even though I had finished *Boy's Life* by Robert McCammon, I still could not shake the **woeful** heaviness I felt after reading about the death in the book.

___d___ **Woeful** means

    a. joyful.   c. fortunate.

    b. careless.   d. sad.

EXERCISE 2   Word Sorts

Synonyms

Match the word to the synonyms or definitions that follow each blank.

1. __woeful_____ heartbreaking; grieving; gloomy; heartrending

2. __ballad_____ narrative; folk tale; song; romance

3. __saw_____ adage; aphorism; saying; proverb

4. __pard_____ large cat; leopard; tiger; jaguar

5. __satchel_____ bag; container; briefcase; suitcase

Antonyms

Select the letter of the word(s) with the opposite meaning.

__a__ **6.** sans
  a. with
  b. outside
  c. absent
  d. without

__c__ **7.** oath
  a. pledge
  b. promise
  c. betrayal
  d. worry

__d__ **8.** mewl
  a. cry
  b. whine
  c. weep
  d. debate

__b__ **9.** treble
  a. shrill sound
  b. whisper
  c. high-pitched sound
  d. slang

__a__ **10.** oblivion
  a. awareness
  b. forgetfulness
  c. emptiness
  d. loss

EXERCISE **3** Fill in the Blank

Use context clues to determine the word that best completes each sentence.

1. James has many friends because he is a man of honor who always keeps his <u>oaths</u>.

2. The <u>woeful</u> sound of the foghorn warning ships in the channel woke Kristy, and the sad tone set her mood for the rest of the day.

3. The movie star was a famous celebrity for one year, and then she mysteriously disappeared into <u>oblivion</u> and was quickly forgotten by her fans.

4. I love looking at the <u>pard</u>(s) in a wildlife sanctuary, but seeing a leopard or tiger in a circus always makes me sad.

5. We gathered around the porch of Uncle John's house and sang <u>ballad</u>(s) while he played the guitar.

6. Whenever the Wicked Witch of the West cackled in her <u>treble</u>, "I'll get you, my pretty!" my baby sister would hide her face with her hands and peek at the TV through a web of fingers.

7. A favorite <u>saw</u> around our house is "Little by little does the trick."

8. When Janie began to <u>mewl</u> about not having enough money to buy new clothes, her father reminded her that she could gain financial autonomy if she found a job.

9. The salesman grabbed his <u>satchel</u> filled with miracle cures and ran to catch the train before his unsatisfied customers could catch up with him.

10. Although many people believe food is plentiful, the food bank seems to be <u>sans</u> supplies since the recent natural disasters used up their stockpile.

EXERCISE 4 Application

Using context clues, insert the vocabulary word in the appropriate blank. A part-of-speech clue is given for each vacabulary word.

On the first day of class of English 241, Dr. Tompkins opened his briefcase, which looked more like a 16th century **(1)** (n.) <u>satchel</u>. "We are about to take a journey into another time," he began. And so it was. Our entire course was like a trip back to Elizabethan England, and our guide was an imaginative, learned professor.

"William Shakespeare," he began, "was born in April of 1564, and by the age of 18 was married to Anne Hathaway in 1582. Together they had three children: Susanna, and twins Judith and Hamnet. Little is known of his wife, except that she was a farmer's daughter, and her first child was born just six months after their marriage, and, oh yes, she was eight years older than her husband."

Murmuring rippled through the lecture hall at those last two comments.

"Yes, well," Professor Tompkins continued, "His wife seems to have disappeared into a kind of **(2)** (n.) oblivion_____, forgotten **(3)** (prep.) sans_____ fanfare, while her husband William, who is now in London, quickly makes a name for himself as writer, poet, and actor. Still, as we will see in a later lecture, Shakespeare maintains a relationship with his children, and slips into a **(4)** (adj.) woeful_____ period of sadness with the death of one of his twins, Hamnet.

"Shakespeare," Professor Tompkins said, "went on to produce 36 plays that we will explore—his comedies and tragedies and histories. When studying these, remember Hamlet's line,

'Give me that man
That is not passion's slave, and I will wear him
In my heart's core, ay, in my heart of heart,
As I do thee.'
Hamlet III, ii

And remember that Shakespeare believed most of men's tragedies resulted from being passion's slave."

At this point someone in the lecture hall squealed in a **(5)** (n.) treble_____, "A smart man!" The comment was then followed by laughter and students nodding in agreement.

Dr. Tompkins laughed. "Ah, yes, well, then we all agree that no matter what time period, there are some things that remain true and constant. For example, what people consider entertaining in Shakespeare's time is no different from now. We enjoy seeing people dressed in disguises, whether as **(6)** (n.) pards_____ or other large cats that **(7)** (v.) mewl_____ under a full moon, and we enjoy stories of old **(8)** (n.) ballads_____ telling of true love, of heroic deeds, of the keeping of **(9)** (n.) oath _____(s) and of grave mistakes that are committed un-consciously, even when people are trying to do the right things. From all of this, ladies and gentlemen, we can learn much. We can even try not to repeat the same mistakes.

"Shakespeare's plays and sonnets have also lasted because they contain nuggets of truth that have been passed on as famous quotes and **(10)** (n.) saw _____(s) — sayings that touch the human heart. For example, most people can quote these lines from *Hamlet*:

'To be or not to be,—that is the question—
Whether 'tis nobler in the mind to suffer
The slings and arrows of outrageous fortune
Or to take arms against a sea of troubles,
And by opposing end them?'– From *Hamlet* (III, i, 56–61)

"Makes one think of the lyrics by The Clash, 'Should I stay or should I go?' doesn't it?" Professor Tompkins concluded, laughing.

We laughed again. With such a good professor, we knew this semester would be a great one.

Stop and Think

 Reread the lines from *As You Like It* in this chapter, and in the space below, write a description of each stage of life presented by Shakespeare. Include one vocabulary word in your description of each stage.

Stage 1	
Stage 2	
Stage 3	
Stage 4	
Stage 5	
Stage 6	
Stage 7	

 Go to **http://www.stratford.co.uk/prop1.asp** to identify the house below. Then write a caption using one of the words from this chapter.

Elizabeth Pongratz

Because this is Shakespeare's

birthplace, it is a house that will

never end up in **oblivion.**

_____

_____

_____

_____

Vocabulary and Humanities

Get Ready to Read About Humanities

The study of humanities includes topics in music, fine arts, world cultures, literature, philosophy, religion, architecture, and even film history. The purpose is to enhance a student's understanding of culture and what makes us human. Most colleges require students to take a humanities course because academicians—people who work in education—believe that an understanding of humanities will develop the "whole" person. Before you read the selection, consider what you have learned about the following word parts.

1. The prefix *com-* means <u>with, together</u>.

2. The root *mort* means *death*.

3. The suffix *-ance* means *state, quality* and indicates a <u>noun</u>.

4. The suffix *-ate* means *cause to become, make* and indicates a <u>verb</u>.

5. The suffix *-tion* means *action; state* and indicates a <u>noun</u>.

| abundance | deity | mortal | placate | ritual |
| compensation | inferior | myth | quarrel | woo |

THE NATURAL WORLD

Many early **myths** were designed to explain nature, and many early **rituals** were efforts to control it. In Scandinavian communities, for example, the fertility **deity** was Freyr, who was thought to bring rich harvests to the earth. He did so by **wooing** a maiden, symbolizing the union of earth and sky. Rituals that honored Freyr and the **abundance** he gave were essential for survival. In almost all early cultures, help from the gods was needed if crops should fail or were insufficient, for then the **mortals** had to turn to the sea where food could be found only if the storm god were **placated.**

According to an Aztec myth, before the universe was formed, there were gods. A fight developed over who would create which part of the world. Eventually a snake divided in half—one half to create the upper part, the other half to create the lower part. The one who created the earth felt that she was less important and began to **quarrel** with the one who created the heavens. As **compensation** for her **inferior** position, the gods added to her importance by allowing different parts of her body to be the source of important elements—the rivers and streams coming from her eyes, for instance.

—Janaro & Altshuler, *The Art of Being Human*, 6th ed., p. 513.

VISUAL VOCABULARY

To __b__ a crying baby, a parent will calm the infant by talking softly, singing lullabies, using finger plays and reciting nursery rhymes for entertainment.

a. quarrel
b. placate

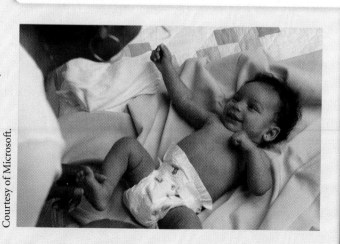

Courtesy of Microsoft.

EXERCISE **1** Context Clues

Refer to the previous passage and use context clues from the sentences below to determine the definition of each of the following words in **bold** print. Do not consult a dictionary.

1. abundance (ə-bŭn′dəns) n.
   At Thanksgiving, Roger's family volunteers to help cook and serve dinner to the homeless who have not experienced the same **abundance** of food that others in the town have.

   ___b___ **Abundance** means
       a. agony.   c. disagreement.
       b. great amount.   d. comfort.

2. compensation (kŏm′pən-sā′shən) n.
   Wilma was offered a bonus as **compensation** for the extra time she volunteered to ensure the company's new project would succeed.

   ___c___ **Compensation** means
       a. observation.   c. payment.
       b. supervision.   d. debt.

3. deity (dē′ĭ-tē, dā′-) n.
   The early Greeks worshipped many **deities**; that is, they had many gods and goddesses whose actions they used to explain natural occurrences in everyday life as well as human behavior.

   ___b___ **Deity** means
       a. explanation.   c. human.
       b. god or goddess. d. Greek city.

4. inferior (ĭn-fîr′ē-ər) adj.
   Because of his honesty, the foreman rejected the **inferior**, cheaper steel and insisted that a better grade be ordered, even though the added cost would reduce profits.

   ___a___ **Inferior** means
       a. substandard.   c. inside.
       b. exceptional.   d. expensive.

5. mortal (môr′tl) n.

Although some superheroes appear able to avoid death, even Superman is a **mortal** because he can be destroyed by Kryptonite.

_____a_____ **Mortal** means

    a. someone who is capable of dying.
    b. someone who will live forever.
    c. a very good person.
    d. someone who is not human.

6. myth (mĭth) n.

Urban legends are not real; instead, they are **myths** created to make people afraid to break rules.

_____d_____ **Myth** means

    a. true story.   c. rule.
    b. law.   d. imaginary tale.

7. placate (plā′kāt′) v.

After wrecking the family car, Emily found a part-time job at a local toy store to help pay for the repairs and **placate** her angry father.

_____c_____ **Placate** means

    a. upset.   c. calm.
    b. order.   d. replace.

8. quarrel (kwôr′əl) v.

People who tend to be peacemakers will go to great lengths to avoid a **quarrel** or a fight with others.

_____b_____ **Quarrel** means

    a. length.   c. understanding.
    b. argument.   d. silence.

9. ritual (rĭch′oo-əl) n.

One American **ritual** is to sing "The Star-Spangled Banner" before each athletic event.

_____a_____ **Ritual** means

    a. tradition.   c. prayer.
    b. game.   d. hard work.

10. woo (wōō) v.

Allen quickly realized he would have to use romantic music, flowers, and poetic words to **woo** the woman of his dreams before she would agree to marry him.

_____a_____ **Woo** means

a. persuade.

b. discourage.

c. hire.

d. avoid.

EXERCISE ② Word Sorts

Synonyms

Match the word to the synonyms or definitions that follow each blank.

1. ritual _____ tradition; ceremony; routine; practice

2. woo _____ court; charm; lure; entice

3. placate _____ soothe; allay; pacify; calm

4. mortal _____ person; individual; human; being

5. inferior _____ poor; mediocre; average; below grade

Antonyms

Select the letter of the word(s) with the opposite meaning.

_____a_____ **6.** compensation

a. penalty

b. award

c. payment

d. insurance

_____c_____ **7.** myth

a. legend

b. memory

c. historical record

d. fairy tale

_____a_____ **8.** quarrel

a. agreement

b. disagreement

c. contract

d. legal document

_____b_____ **9.** abundance

a. plenty

b. lack

c. source

d. enough

_____d_____ **10.** deity

a. god

b. goddess

c. immortal

d. human

EXERCISE **3** Fill in the Blank

Use context clues to determine the word that best completes each sentence.

1. Many people believe that the high salary of a professional athlete is fair
   <u>compensation</u> for the physical hardship he or she endures.

2. Mary begins each day with the same <u>ritual</u>: coffee while she
   has her oatmeal; coffee while she rides the bus and reads the newspaper;
   coffee while she reads her e-mail.

3. Men who feel weak and <u>inferior</u> frequently surround themselves with powerful, intelligent women.

4. One famous Egyptian <u>deity</u> was Re, creator of all things.

5. "It is a gift to be <u>mortal</u>," said our philosophy professor, "because our limited number of days makes us appreciate the joyous moments."

6. "A good vocabulary in a man is so sexy," said Jessica, who admitted that a
   rich range of words could <u>woo</u> her more than a dozen roses.

7. Going into a job interview with an <u>abundance</u> of confidence is one
   key to getting the job of your dreams.

8. To <u>placate</u> his demanding boss, David agreed to work week-
   ends, knowing such a plan would not please his wife.

9. Although the customer seemed ready to begin a <u>quarrel</u>, the
   salesclerk remained professional and friendly, remembering that arguing
   with the public was against company policy.

10. If you study the <u>myth</u>(s) of ancient civilizations, you can be-
    gin to understand what they held as important and start to unravel the
    mysteries of people who lived long ago.

EXERCISE **4** Application

Using context clues, insert the vocabulary word in the appropriate blank. A
part-of-speech clue is given for each vocabulary word.

All cultures have **(1)** (n.) <u>myth</u>(s), or legends, that are

central to their beliefs. Some stories explain natural occurrences such as the

changing of seasons or the moods of the seas. Others teach lessons to encourage citizens to make good choices or show compassion, or to explain the

(2) (n.) _ritual_____ (s) and traditions of their times.

In Greek mythology, for example, one story is about the

(3) (n.) _deity_____ Persephone, who was goddess of the under-

world. Instead of trying to **(4)** (v.) _woo_____ her, Hades, the god of

the underworld, kidnapped the beautiful and beloved daughter of Zeus and

Demeter, the goddess of the harvest. Knowing that his world was

(5) (adj.) _inferior_____ to her light-filled one, he believed that stealing

her was the only way to win her. When Demeter learned that her daughter

had fallen through a hole in the earth while she was delighting in some beau-

tiful flowers, she became depressed. As a result, the fields were no longer fer-

tile and the harvest was no longer filled with the **(6)** (adj.) _abundance_____

of fruit and vegetables and wheat that the world experienced in the past. Thus

winter occurred. To **(7)** (v.) _placate_____ Demeter, Hades allowed

Persephone to go back home. However, because she ate the seeds of a pome-

granate he had given to her, she was cursed to return to the underworld for

one-third of each year. Hence, the Greeks had an explanation for the seasons.

Another Greek myth is the story of a **(8)** (n.) _mortal_____

named Narcissus. Unlike the gods, Narcissus was human. However, he was so

handsome that he began to feel overly proud of his attractiveness, believing

he was almost godlike. Although some **(9)** (v.) _quarrel_____ over the

believability of the story, which has several versions, many agree that because

of his excessive pride, Narcissus stared lovingly at his own reflection in a pool

of water, where he eventually drowned. As **(10)** (n.) _compensation_____ for

his death, slender flowers with delicate white blossoms grew at the edge of the

pool. Ironically, these were the same flowers that Persephone was admiring

when Hades stole her away from earth.

Stop and Think

 Go to **www.wikipedia.org** and search the definitions of the following words. Then complete the sentence.

1. narcissistic/ Narcissistic people are focused mainly on <u>themselves</u>.

2. phobia/ A phobia of adolescents gaining more rights is called <u>ephebophobia</u>.

3. atlas/ King Altas supposedly made the first <u>celestial globe</u>.

 Select three words from the chapter and complete the boxes below by writing the word and a synonym, and then drawing a picture that represents it.

Word	Synonym	Picture

18

Vocabulary and Music Appreciation

Get Ready to Read About Music Appreciation

Music appreciation is a specialized humanities course that focuses on the history and development of various genres, or categories, of music. Also, it presents the qualities and key vocabulary words associated with those categories of music. Before you read the following selection, consider the word parts you will encounter.

1. The prefix *de-* means *down, from, away.*

2. The prefix *con-* means *with, together.*

3. The prefix *mille-* means *thousand.*

4. The prefix *per-* means *through.*

5. The prefix *un-* means <u>not</u>.

6. The root *claim* means *to cry out.*

7. The root *enn* means <u>year</u>.

8. The root *nomen* means <u>name</u>.

9. The root *temp* means *time.*

10. The suffix *-ible* means *capable of* and indicates an <u>adjective</u>.

| acclaim | contemporary | era | millennium | phenomenon |
| bellow | denounce | facet | pervasive | unintelligible |

ROCK

Rock, known variously as rock'n roll, rock & roll, and rock and roll, has been such a **pervasive phenomenon** during the second half of the twentieth century that it surely belongs in a humanities text. Both **acclaimed** and **denounced** on all sides since it made the scene in the 1950s, rock has become a major way of defining in sound our **era** in history. There is little doubt it will survive well into the current **millennium.**

Though it has many complex **facets,** ranging from the conscious artistry of trained musicians to the out-of-control **bellowing** of **unintelligible** lyrics by performers prancing around a stage, rock is first and foremost a celebration of the joy of life, of sexual release, of total disregard for social rules.

As a **contemporary** musical form, rock realizes its full potential in the rock concert, in a given totality of work presented in a unique program that is almost never repeated after a particular performance on tour.

—Janaro & Altshuler, *The Art of Being Human*, 6th ed., p. 246.

VISUAL VOCABULARY

Sometimes ___b___ sculptures decorate a city and provide modern artwork in an ordinary setting such as a park.

a. pervasive
b. contemporary

George Pongratz

EXERCISE 1 Context Clues

Refer to the previous passage and use context clues from the sentences below to determine the definition of each of the following words in **bold** print. Do not consult a dictionary.

1. acclaim (ə-klām′) n.
   Even though the film received worldwide **acclaim** from movie critics, poor box office sales proved the fans did not agree with their approval.

   __a__ **Acclaim** means
   - a. praise.
   - b. consequence.
   - c. money.
   - d. global criticism.

2. bellow (bĕl′ō) v.
   We nicknamed our math teacher Ms. Thunderlungs because on the first day of class, she **bellowed** at us in a booming and frightening voice, "You will not even breathe in this room without my permission."

   __b__ **Bellow** means
   - a. whisper gently.
   - b. shout in a loud voice.
   - c. whine pitifully.
   - d. request respectfully.

3. contemporary (kən-tĕm′pə-rĕr′ē) adj.
   Ben's sister used to listen to **contemporary** music only, but after taking a music appreciation class her freshman year, she now prefers to study with classical music in the background.

   __a__ **Contemporary** means
   - a. modern.
   - b. old-fashioned.
   - c. past.
   - d. professional.

4. denounce (dĭ-nouns′) v.
   The newly elected parliament **denounced** the old form of government, and instead announced their preference for a democracy led by officials elected by the country's citizens.

   __c__ **Denounce** means
   - a. praise.
   - b. ignore.
   - c. criticize.
   - d. make stable.

5. facet (făs′ĭt) n.

The job of an investigative journalist has many **facets**: detailed research, constant networking of sources, seeking truth, composing an accurate story without bias, and working under pressure in a short period of time.

___c___ **Facet** means

    a. career.   c. part.

    b. search.   d. story.

6. era (îr′ə, ĕr′ə) n.

We are in an **era** in which many of the "hot" jobs include physical therapist, occupational therapist, computer systems analyst, nurse, and teacher, but we will also need engineers to replace the experienced scientists who are retiring.

___d___ **Era** means

    a. market.   c. need.

    b. field.   d. period.

7. millennium (mə-lĕn′ē-əm)n.

This new **millennium** offers exciting hope of cures for serious, life-threatening diseases, as well as changes for the environment such as global warming and a loss of natural resources.

___b___ **Millennium** means

    a. new cure.   c. a new decade.

    b. a span of a thousand years. d. a new century.

8. pervasive (pər-vā′sĭv) adj.

"While the threat of terrorism becomes more **pervasive**, we must be careful to preserve our civil liberties," cautioned the presidential candidate.

___d___ **Pervasive** means

    a. cautious.   c. rare.

    b. popular.   d. widespread.

9. phenomenon (fĭ-nŏm′ə-nŏn′) n.

When the freshman quarterback was sent in to replace the injured senior, the fans were amazed by the new **phenomenon**—a fast, graceful touchdown machine.

___d___ **Phenomenon** means

    a. disappointment.   c. beginner.

    b. veteran.   d. wonder.

10. unintelligible (ŭn´ĭn-tĕl´ĭ-jə-bəl) adj.

After the stranger was found wandering the streets, cold, hungry, dirty, mumbling **unintelligible** sentences, and carrying no identification, a concerned bystander walked him to a nearby restaurant for food and warmth, and then called 911.

___d___ **Unintelligible** means

a. well-formed.	c. flowery.
b. sensible.	d. unclear.

EXERCISE 2 Word Sorts

Synonyms

Match the word to the synonyms or definitions that follow each blank.

1. pervasive_____ prevalent; widespread; ubiquitous; extensive

2. facet_____ feature; part; angle; element

3. denounce_____ criticize; condemn; impugn; accuse

4. era_____ period; age; generation; time

5. millennium_____ thousand years; future; eternity; morrow

Antonyms

Select the letter of the word(s)with the opposite meaning.

___d___ **6.** contemporary

a. beautiful	c. modern
b. simple	d. old

___b___ **7.** acclaim

a. praise	c. applause
b. disapproval	d. attention

___c___ **8.** phenomenon

a. marvel	c. disappointment
b. amazement	d. newcomer

___a___ **9.** bellow

a. whisper	c. yell
b. shout	d. discuss

_____a_____ **10.** unintelligible
     a. clear   c. unclear
     b. vague   d. cloudy

EXERCISE **3** Fill in the Blank

Use context clues to determine the word that best completes each sentence.

1. During this new _millennium_ we will we see more fuel-efficient cars such as hybrids and those that use biofuels.

2. One _facet_, or aspect, of marketing research involves an understanding of psychology and of what attracts people to one product rather than another.

3. The _acclaim_ the candidate received during his campaign made people predict that he would win the popular vote in the country.

4. _Contemporary_ architecture is often a display of glass, steel, simple lines, and little clutter.

5. During her film studies class, Ruth Ann revealed that her favorite scene is in *A Streetcar Named Desire* when Marlon Brando _bellows_, "Stella!"

6. When the Supreme Court nominee was _denounced_ by even conservative members of Congress, she withdrew her name from consideration.

7. As a result of some current research, the appearance of medical centers that focus on the heart and brain connection suggest that we are moving into an _era_ where even scientists recognize a relationship between the mind and body.

8. Learning to communicate more effectively in college will help you avoid writing _unintelligible_ letters, memos, directives, and reports once you are in your career.

9. "Apathy, or the lack of concern, has become a _pervasive_ problem," observed the mayor, "and we need to find a way to generate more enthusiasm that will spread throughout the community."

10. The new swimming _phenomenon_ surprised the Olympic judges, who were filled with amazement when he completed the trials and was quickly on the deck waiting for the rest of the athletes to finish the event.

EXERCISE **4** Application

Using context clues, insert the vocabulary word in the appropriate blank. A part-of-speech clue is given for each vacabulary word.

At a time when many people search for heroes and **(1)** (v.) denounce _____ most miracles as jokes or frauds, at least one **(2)** (n.) phenomenon _____ that has generated amazement and wide **(3)** (n.) acclaim _____ is an antique light bulb that has burned continuously since it was first given to the firefighters of Station 6 in Livermore, California, in 1901. This is a delightful mystery in an **(4)** (n.) era _____ when people's suspicions of the unexplainable are **(5)** (adj.) pervasive _____ and widespread throughout the world. Unlike **(6)** (adj.) contemporary _____ light bulbs, this 4-watt, hand-blown bulb with a carbide filament has baffled G.E. engineers. No one understands why it has not burned out.

Until it was authenticated in 1972, firefighters were careless around the light bulb. However, when they learned of its significance and true age, everyone become more careful. For example, it has been mounted high enough so that it is out of damage range. Damaging the prized bulb now would probably prompt the firefighters to **(7)** (v.) bellow _____ in protests and shout **(8)** (adj.) unintelligible _____ phrases because it has become something people cherish.

The mystery has many aspects. One **(9)** (n.) facet _____ is that the bulb illuminates an area over the firefighters' equipment, and another is that it has only been turned off once; when the fire station was relocated in 1976, it was gently transported in a foam-enclosed box. Called the "Centennial Bulb," it burned through the entire 20th century and has continued to work into the next **(10)** (n.) ‾‾millennium‾‾‾‾‾‾‾. "I think it will burn

for another 100 years," said one optimistic firefighter.

Source: http://www.centennialbulb.org/

Stop and Think

Go to **www.http://www.centennialbulb.org/** to see a picture of the Centennial Bulb. Then choose one vocabulary word from this chapter to summarize the story of the bulb and explain your reason for that choice.

One word summary:_____

_____

_____

Finish the following to make a complete sentence that reveals the definition of the word.

1. A **pervasive** problem on college campuses that we should address and

   work to fix is _____

   _____.

2. One thing I look forward in this new **millennium** is _____

   _____.

3. The one time I was so nervous that my words were **unintelligible** was

   when I _____

   _____.

4. An amazing **phenomenon** I would like to witness is _____

   _____.

5. A movie I have seen that deserved the critics' **acclaim** is _____

   _____.

Review Test
Chapters 15–18

1 Word Parts

Match the definitions in Column 2 to the word parts in Column 1.

Column 1

Column 2

j   **1.** mille-

a. two

e   **2.** enn

b. cry out

b   **3.** claim

c. able to

i   **4.** nomen

d. carry

g   **5.** temp

e. year

h   **6.** mort

f. like; resembling

c   **7.** -ible

g. time

f   **8.** -al

h. death

d   **9.** fer

i. name

a   **10.** bi-

j. thousand

5

2 Fill in the Blank

Use context clues to determine the best word from the box to complete each sentence.

ballad	denounce	inter	oath	quarrel
confront	facet	myth	pard	satchel

1. In some cultures a _pard_____ is considered an animal of good luck.

2. "Keeping all of your e-mails in your computer in-box is like stuffing all of your mail back in your business _satchel_____," warned the organization expert.

3. To _confront_____ the problem of homelessness in our city, many churches have united to take turns housing and feeding those in need during the winter months.

4. After lying in state in the Capitol Rotunda in Washington, D.C., the body of Rosa Parks was _inter_____(red) next to her husband at a Detroit cemetery.

5. One of Johnny Cash's hits was the "_Ballad_____ of Ira Hayes"—the story of a Pima Indian who became a Marine hero, but later died, abandoned and alone.

6. When immigrants become naturalized citizens, they take a(n) _oath_____ to support the ideals of the constitution.

7. As a part of his health plan, the doctor tried to educate his patients and explain that it was a _myth_____ that a person would burn more calories if he slept fewer hours a night, because, in reality, a person who wants to lose weight needs at least eight hours of sleep.

8. Billy Collins's poem, "Another Reason Why I Don't Own a Gun," is about his enduring the sounds of a neighbor's barking dog, rather than _quarrel_____ with a friend.

9. Citizens _denounce_____(d) the city's transportation plan as shortsighted and without a vision of future growth.

5

10. One <u>facet</u> of the new program is to provide scholarships for students who maintain a 3.0 average and participate in community service.

3 Book Connection

Use context clues to determine the best word from the box to complete each sentence.

abundance	adjust	deity	oblivion	ritual
acclaim	authority	engage	phenomenon	woeful

TUESDAYS WITH MORRIE

When author Mitch Albom learned that his former college professor, Morrie Schwartz, was ill, he went to Schwartz's home to reconnect with him. The visit led to many other visits as well as Schwartz's request that Albom draft a book that would teach people how to live full lives while observing Morrie as he moves closer to death. Each visit became a **(1)** <u>ritual</u> that provided the two men with opportunities to **(2)** <u>engage</u> in discussions on love and friendship and work. As the teacher and figure of **(3)** <u>authority</u>, Morrie had lived a rich and meaningful life, not just as a spectator, but as a true participant. He was learning to **(4)** <u>adjust</u> to the idea of dying.

When he was diagnosed with ALS, Morrie was initially stunned. However, he began to focus on his situation, not as a **(5)** <u>woeful</u> condition, but rather as an opportunity to help others appreciate the **(6)** <u>abundance</u> and simplicity of the human experience. Because of their friendship and Albom's book, Morrie Schwartz will never disappear into **(7)** <u>oblivion</u>. Instead, since his death and the publishing of the book, Morrie occupies a place in the memories and lives of thousands of readers.

5

The book won immediate worldwide **(8)** <u>acclaim</u> and has been regarded as a publishing **(9)** <u>phenomenon</u>. While people can read quickly through the little book as a tender true story, many choose to read a chapter a night and then think deeply about each subject, whether it is about a personal **(10)** <u>diety</u> who watches over each of us, our connection to family and friends, or how we should conduct ourselves on our human journey. The gist of the message is love—something we see in the friendship the author nurtures with his special professor as well as the relationship Morrie has with his wife and community of support. Ultimately, we learn to savor moments and remember to tell those we love how much they mean to us.

4 Visual Connection

Write a caption for this picture using two words from the box. (Answers will vary.)

ballad	compensation	oath	relational	sole
bellow	inferior	oration	sans	treble

George Pongratz

_____

_____

_____

_____

_____

_____

_____

_____

5 Analogies

Choose the word that best completes the analogy.

1. anger : argue :: persuade : ___b___
   a. ignore   b. woo   c. conclude

2. attentive : focused :: widespread : ___b___
   a. contemporary   b. pervasive   c. literal

3. hint : suggestion :: conclusion : ___c___
   a. question   b. millennium   c. inference

4. hard-boiled : thick-skinned :: easily hurt : ___a___
   a. sensitive   b. mortal   c. factual

5. giggle : cry :: laugh : ___b___
   a. placate   b. mewl   c. conclude

6. saying : motto :: proverb : ___a___
   a. saw   b. order   c. era

7. alive : dead :: immortal : ___b___
   a. factual   b. mortal   c. contemporary

8. frustrate : satisfy :: anger : ___b___
   a. mewl   b. placate   c. suggest

9. furniture : antique :: architecture : ___a___
   a. contemporary   b. factual   c. bias

10. certain : unclear :: clear : ___a___
   a. unintelligible   b. phenomenon   c. contemporary

Word Parts

Roots

Root	Meaning	Example
alter	change	altercation
ama	love	amorous
anima	breath, spirit	animated
anno	year	annual
aqua	water	aquifer
aster, astro	star	asteroid
aud	hear	auditory
bene	good	beneficial
bio	life	biology
cap	head	decapitate
cap, capt	take	captivate
card, cor, cord	heart	cardiologist, core
ced, ceed, cess	go	proceed
cosmo	order, universe	cosmos
cresc	grow, increase	crescendo
cryp	secret, hidden	crypt
dent	tooth	dentist
derm	skin	epidermis
dict	say	predict
duc, duct	lead, guide	conductor
dynam	power	dynamic
ego	self	egotistical
equ, equal	equal	equilibrium
err, errat	wander	erratic
ethno	race, tribe	ethnic
fac, fact	do, make	factory
fer	carry	transfer
flu, fluct, flux	flow	influx
fract	break	fracture
frater	brother	fraternal
gene	race, kind, sex	genetics

Root	Meaning	Example
grad, gres	go, take, steps	graduate
graph	write, draw	autograph
gyn	woman	gynecologist
hab, habi	have, hold	habitat
hap	change	happenstance
helio	sun, light	heliograph
ject	throw	eject
lat	carry	translate
lic, liqu, list	leave behind	liquidate
lith	stone	monolith
loc	place	relocate
log	speech, science, reason	logic
loquor	speak	colloquial
lumen, lumin	light	luminary
macro	large	macroeconomics
manu	hand	manual
mater	mother	maternal
med	middle	mediator
meter	measure	thermometer
micro	small	microorganism
miss, mit	send, let go	transmit
morph	form	morpheme
mort	die	mortal
mot, mov	movement	demote
mut, muta	change	mutation
nat	be born	natural, native
neg, negat	say no, deny	negate, negative
nomen, nym	name	antonym, synonym
pel, puls	push, drive	propel
philo	love	philanthropy
ocul	eye	monocle
ortho	right, straight	orthodontist
osteo	bone	osteoporosis
pater	father	paternal
path	suffering, feeling	pathology
ped	child	pediatrician
ped, pod	foot	podiatrist
phobia	fear	claustrophobia
phon	sound	telephone
photo	light	photograph
plic	fold	implicate

Root	Meaning	Example
pneuma	wind, air	pneumonia
pon, pos, posit	put, place	dispose
port	carry	import
pseudo	false	pseudonym
psych	mind	psychology
press	press	compress
pyr	fire	pyromaniac
quir, quis	ask	inquire
rog	question	interrogate
scope	see	microscope
scrib, script	write	inscription
sect	cut	dissect
sequi	follow	sequence
sol	alone	solitude
soma	body	somatotype
somnia	sleep	insomnia
soph	wise	sophisticated
soror	sister	sorority
spect	look	inspect
spers	scatter	disperse
spir	breathe	inspire
struct	build	construction
tact	touch	tactile
tain, tent	hold	contain
tempo	time	temporary
the, theo	God	theology
therm	heat	thermometer
tort	twist	contort
tract	drag, pull	extract
verbum	word	verbatim
vis	see	revise

Prefixes

Prefix	Meaning	Example
a-, ab-	away, from	abduct
a-, an-	not, without	asexual
ac-, ad-	to, toward	accept, admit
ambi-, amphi-	both, around	ambivalent, amphitheater

Prefix	Meaning	Example
ante-	in front of, before	antecedent
anti-	against, oppose	antisocial
auto-	self	automatic
bi-	two, twice	bifocal
cata-, cath-	down, downward	catacombs
cent-	hundred	centennial
chrono-	time	chronological
circum-	around	circumspect
col-, com-, con-	with, together	collate, combine, connection
contra-	against	contradict
de-	down away, reversal	destruction
deca-	ten	decade
demi-	half	demigod
di-, duo-	two	dioxide
dia-	between, through	diagonal, dialogue
dis-	apart, away, in different directions	dismiss
dys-	ill, hard	dysfunctional
e-, ex-	out, from	emerge, expel
epi-	on, near, among	epidemic
eu-	good	euphoric
extra-	beyond, outside	extramarital
hecto-	hundred	hectogram
hemi-	half	hemisphere
hetero-	other, different	heterosexual
homo-	same	homonym
hyper-	above, excessive	hyperactive
hypo-	under	hypodermic
il-, im-, in-	not	illogical, impossible
im-, in-	in, into, on	implant, inject
infra-	lower	infrastructure
inter-	between, among	intercede
intra-	within	intranet
iso-	equal	isometric
juxta-	next to	juxtapose
mal-	wrong, ill	malpractice

Prefix	Meaning	Example
meta-	about	metaphysical
micro-	small	microscope
mil-	thousand	millennium
mis-	wrong	mistake
mono-	one	monotone
multi-	many	multimedia
non-	not	nonactive
nona-	nine	nonagon
octo-	eight	octopus
omni-	all	omniscient
pan-	all	panorama
penta-	five	pentagram
per-	through	pervade
peri-	around	periscope
poly-	many	polygon
post-	after, behind	postscript
pre-	before	precede
pro-	forward, on behalf of	promote
proto-	first	prototype
quadri-	four	quadrant
quint-	five	quintuplets
re-	back, again	retract
retro-	backward	retrospect
semi-	half	semicircle
sesqui-	one and a half	sesquicentennial
sex-	six	sextet
sub-, sup-	under, from below	subgroup, support
super-	above, over, beyond	supervise
sym-, syn-	together, with	symmetry, synonym
tele-	far, from a distance	telegraph
tetra-	four	tetrahedron
trans-	across	transport
tri-	three	triangle, triplet
ultra-	excessive, beyond	ultrasonic
un-	not	unnecessary
uni-	one	uniform
vice-	in place of	viceroy

Suffixes

Suffix	Meaning	Example
Noun suffixes	*People, places, thing*	
-acle, -acy, -ance	quality, state	privacy
-an	of, related to	American
-ant, -ary	one who, one that	servant
-arium, -ary	place or container	auditorium
-ation	action, process	education
-ator	one who	spectator
-cide	kill	homicide
-eer, -er, -ess	person, doer	collector
-ence, -ency	quality, state	residence, residency
-ent	one who, one that	president
-hood	quality, condition, state	brotherhood
-ician	specialist	statistician
-ism	belief	modernism
-ist	person	extremist
-ity	quality, trait	sincerity
-logy	study of	biology
-ment	act, state	statement
-ness	quality, condition, state	illness
-or	person, doer	juror
-path	practitioner; sufferer of a disorder	osteopath; psychopath
-ship	quality, condition, state	relationship
-tion	action, state	fraction
-tude	quality, degree	multitude
-y	quality, trait	apathy
Adjective suffixes	*Descriptions of nouns*	
-able	capable of	reusable
-ac, -al, -an, -ar, -ative	of, like, related to, being	logical
-ent	of, like, related to, being	persistent
-ful	full of	fearful
-ible	capable of	defensible
-ic, -ical, -ile, -ious, -ish, -ive	of, like, related to, being	feverish
-less	without	luckless

B

Foreign Words and Phrases

While many words in your dictionary evolved from Greek and Latin word parts, some word have remained intact from their original form. These foreign words and phrases will appear in your everyday use as well as in some academic settings.

French

1. á la carte (ä′ lə kärt′ə) adv., adj. [by the bill of fare] a menu list that prices each item separately

2. cul-de-sac (kŭl də săk) n. [bottom of the bag] a dead end

3. déjà vu (dā′zhävoo′) n. [already seen] the sensation that you have heard or done something before

Latin

4. in loc parentis (ĭn lō′kō pə-rĕn′tĭs) adv. [in place of parents] supervision by an administration such as a university acting in place of the parents

5. pro bono (prō bō′nō) adj. [for the public good] donating professional services for the public good

6. quid pro quo (kwĭd′ prō kwō′) n. [something for something] something given or received for something else; an equal exchange

Italian

7. finale (fə-năl′ē) n. [final] the last section in a performance

Spanish

8. bonanza (bə-năn′zə) n. [calm sea] a large amount

9. bravado (bra-väd-o) n. [bragging] bragging, boastful action; a false show of bravery

10. renegade (rĕn′ĭ-gād′) n. [to deny] someone who refuses to act in a lawful or traditional manner

Partial Answer Key

Chapter 1

Practice 1A

1. b
2. a
3. c
4. c
5. a

Practice 2A

1. c
2. a
3. b
4. d
5. a

Practice 3A

1. d
2. a
3. b
4. a
5. d

Practice 4A

1. d
2. a
3. a
4. b
5. d

Practice 5

1. c
2. a
3. b
4. c
5. a

Chapter 2
Exercise 1

1. a
2. b
3. b
4. b
5. b

6. a
7. b
8. a
9. a
10. a

Chapter 3

1. c
2. a
3. d
4. a
5. b
6. a
7. b
8. c
9. c
10. a

Chapter 4

1. b
2. c

3. a
4. d
5. b
6. a
7. c
8. a
9. d
10. b

Chapter 5

1. b
2. d
3. a
4. a
5. c
6. c
7. a
8. b
9. c
10. b

Chapter 6

1. b
2. d
3. c
4. a
5. c
6. b
7. b
8. d
9. a
10. a

Chapter 7

1. d
2. c
3. a
4. a
5. d
6. b
7. b
8. c
9. c
10. b

Chapter 8

1. d
2. c
3. b
4. b
5. a

6. c
7. a
8. d
9. d
10. c

Chapter 9

1. c
2. a
3. b
4. b
5. d
6. c
7. d
8. a
9. c
10. a

Chapter 10

1. d
2. a
3. a
4. b
5. c
6. b
7. a
8. d
9. d
10. a

Chapter 11

1. a
2. b
3. b
4. c
5. d
6. a
7. b
8. b
9. d
10. a

Chapter 12

1. b
2. a
3. d
4. c
5. a
6. a
7. c
8. b
9. c
10. b

Chapter 13

1. b
2. a
3. a
4. c

5. d
6. b
7. c
8. c
9. b
10. d

Chapter 14

1. c
2. a
3. a
4. b
5. d
6. b
7. c
8. b
9. d
10. a

Chapter 15

1. c
2. b
3. a
4. a
5. b
6. c
7. d
8. a
9. b
10. c

Chapter 16	Chapter 17	Chapter 18
1. b	1. b	1. a
2. a	2. c	2. b
3. d	3. b	3. a
4. d	4. a	4. c
5. a	5. a	5. c
6. b	6. d	6. d
7. c	7. c	7. b
8. d	8. b	8. d
9. b	9. a	9. d
10. d	10. a	10. d